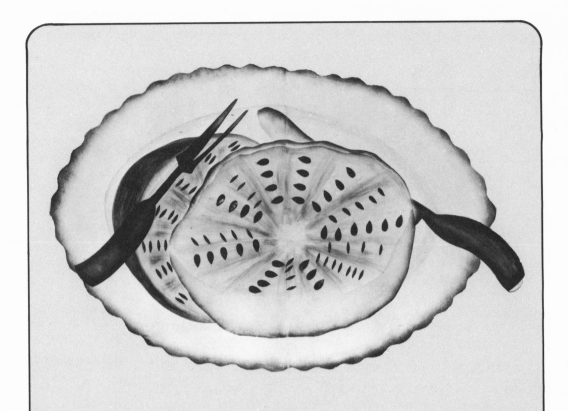

Watermelon. Artist unknown. American, watercolor, c. 1840. *Courtesy Abby Aldrich Rockefeller Folk Art Collection, Williamsburg, Virginia.*

HUNG, STRUNG, AND POTTED

Hung, Strung, & Potted

A History of Eating in Colonial America
by Sally Smith Booth

 Clarkson N. Potter, Inc./Publisher NEW YORK

DISTRIBUTED BY CROWN PUBLISHERS, INC.

Acknowledgments

Grateful acknowledgment is made for permission to reprint quotes from the following:

Narratives of Early Maryland, 1633-1684. Edited by Clayton C. Hall. New York: Barnes and Noble, Inc., 1959.

The Prose Works of William Byrd of Westover. Edited by Louis B. Wright. Cambridge: The Belknap Press of Harvard University Press, 1966.

A Brief and True Report Concerning Williamsburg in Virginia, by Rutherford Goodwin. Williamsburg: Colonial Williamsburg, Inc., 1959. Reprinted by permission of The Colonial Williamsburg Foundation.

Adams Family Correspondence. Edited by L. H. Butterfield. Vol. 1. Cambridge: The Belknap Press of Harvard University Press, 1963.

Gentleman's Progress. Edited by Carl Bridenbaugh. Chapel Hill: University of North Carolina Press, 1948. Published for The Institute of Early American History and Culture.

Offbeat History: A Compendium of Lively Americana. Edited by Bulkley S. Griffin. Copyright © 1967 by Bulkley Southworth Griffin. Reprinted by permission of The World Publishing Company.

American Cookery, by Amelia Simmons. A facsimile of the first (1796) edition, with an essay from Mary T. Wilson, 1958. Courtesy of the American Antiquarian Society.

To L.P.L. and J.S.J.

Contents

Preface

Cooking was a major chore for the colonial woman. Often a wife in the sixteenth, seventeenth, or eighteenth century had to be a combination hunter, trapper, farmer, fire fighter, weight lifter, and woodchopper just to get dinner on the board. Food preparation was of vital importance to all members of the colonial family, for in these rugged days, survival often depended upon the talents and knowledge of the expert in the kitchen. The difference between life and death may have depended upon the judgment of wives who decided at what period tainted food became inedible, or how much meat to preserve for the cold winter.

Food crops and animals were woven intricately into the lives of pioneers, not only because they provided bodily subsistence, but because other basic necessities came from the earth and forests. Hides for clothing were necessary in the woods where briars and thorns quickly destroyed more fragile cloth garments. Animal hooves were ground for gunpowder, tail hairs were strung for sieves and strainers, and vegetables, such as corn, were used to pay taxes and for trade with the Indians.

Ironically, perhaps no area has been so neglected by scholars as the eating habits of young America. The colonists' clothing, housing, political beliefs, and even sexual practices have long been subjects for commentary. But their choice of food has been greatly neglected.

Those few references that are available usually give a distorted view of colonial eating, for they emphasize the glamorous fare of a small number of wealthy patriots. While prosperous citizens such as George Washington and Benjamin Franklin did indeed enjoy lavish dinners of imported dainties, a thousand times their number supped on mushes of hog's jowl and greens.

European explorers land in Florida at Port Royal and Saint Helen's Island. German engraving from *Brevis Narratio,* 1591. *Photo courtesy Library of Congress.*

Also forgotten are the meals of great numbers of slaves—both black and Indian—together with indentured servants who were not free to roam the nation's forests for food. However, their daily fare of corn bread, sweet potatoes, or snake is as much a part of America's heritage as the succulent banquets of the gentry.

This is not a cookbook, but recipes of the period are included, for the dishes reveal much about the customs and habits of the period. The recipes have not been tested or adapted for present-day use, but are presented with the original early American cooking methods and ingredients. Some of these involve techniques that are now considered unsanitary and dangerous, such as the long periods that food was kept before eating or the use of questionable ingredients like ground seashells. These practices, however, provide valuable clues to the causes of the almost constant digestive ills and frequent deaths from food poisoning that plagued newcomers to the land.

Millions of citizens will help America celebrate her two hundredth birthday in 1976. While the democratic ideals and writings of revolutionary settlers seem strangely modern, their food habits are quite alien. With all the problems, hazards, and stomachaches, this is the story of food in colonial America.

HUNG, STRUNG, AND POTTED

Introduction

When European colonists first landed in America they found not only Indians, virgin lands, and an alien style of life, but the world's largest outdoor supermarket.

Ducks, geese, and pigeons by the millions filled the skies. Forests abounded with deer, hare, squirrels, and quail. In rivers and on seashores thrived giant shad, eels, mussels, lobsters five feet long, and crabs said to be big enough to feed four men each. Trees hung heavy with wild fruits and berries. Vegetables, such as potatoes, squash, corn, and pumpkin, covered the rolling meadows.

But the prices were high for shopping in America's forests and streams. Nearly half of the Pilgrims in Plymouth Colony died during the first year of settlement, while more than two hundred kinds of edible fish flourished in nearby Massachusetts Bay. To the south, the Jamestown area of Virginia boasted great wild turkeys weighing as much as fifty pounds each, foot-long oysters, and gigantic clams. Yet during the 1609 ''Starving Time,'' nine out of ten pioneers died, and the remainder survived on a daily ration that included a few kernels of parched corn, supplemented by ants, rats, and boot leather.

These colonists starved simply because in a country where survival came from living off the land, they were not hunters or fishermen. Plymouth's founders had been city-dwelling Englishmen, accustomed to purchasing and not pursuing their food. Hooks, lines, and traps were as foreign to them as was the court of King James. Adventurers in the ill-fated Jamestown settlement had consistently occupied themselves in the search for gold and other precious cargos instead of storing food for use during the winter famine.

Little support was coming from patrons in the Old World. English ships arriving at both Plymouth and Jamestown provided no relief from hunger, for

1

these small vessels were tightly packed with additional pioneers and had little room for transporting bulky foodstuffs. To early Americans, Britain's great merchant fleet, which had long provided a lifeline to English colonies through-out the world, was merely a one-way conveyor belt bringing extra mouths to ravage the food supplies of already starving villagers.

In the end, early settlers survived not by hacking away the forests to cultivate neat rows of garden vegetables or by domesticating herds of animals in the European manner, but by adopting the hunting and tracking techniques of the Indians. Rather than taming the wilds, these first frontiersmen adjusted their own way of life to conquer the challenges of an alien but abundant land. By the late seventeenth century, however, most settlers had learned from tragic experience how to solve their food-gathering problems. Great numbers of colonists were producing a wide variety of foodstuffs suited to their new country's soil and climate. Gradually, a pattern of eating habits evolved that remained relatively stable until after the Revolutionary War one hundred years later. Basically, the pattern was that most Americans ate enormous quan-tities of the same types of foods. But perhaps never before had any country included the diverse cooking and eating habits that young America exhibited during its early days.

Economic conditions played a major role in this diversity. After 1650, the establishment of a tobacco culture had created a small landed class of planta-tion owners in the South whose wealth matched that of the English aristocracy. Other colonists made great fortunes in shipping from northern port cities such as Boston, New York, and Philadelphia. An enriched merchant class began to emerge in urban areas up and down the Atlantic seaboard. All the ingredients for fine cuisine were available to this new American gentry whose eating habits were shaped by frequent journeys to Europe and by imported British publica-tions that described the newest delicacies.

Like his British counterpart, the American lord's table was stocked with the finest French champagnes, potted swan, and succulent beef, spiced with the best products of the Orient. Meals in these American manor houses were opulent and staggering in variety.

One rung down the colonial economic ladder was a less affluent class composed of clergymen, store owners, small landholders, craftsmen, and plan-tation managers. This early middle class was financially able to purchase a limited amount of imported food and wine, but unlike the wealthiest colonials did not retain full-time servant cooks for the preparation of their meals.

Middle-class board was abundant but not exotic. Most vegetables were home-grown, meats domesticated, and fowl bagged in nearby woods.

Finally, nature was the prime food supplier for great numbers of the colonists. This group included indentured servants, poorest farm laborers, slaves, and backwoodsmen who, like the Indians, were almost completely dependent upon the land for survival. And there were many of these people.

Hardships and deprivations in old Europe made indentured servitude a popular escape for thousands of workmen hoping to move up in the freer American society. In the late 1600s, Virginia's population of fifty thousand included six thousand indentured servants, according to one estimate. During the same period, the majority of all adults in Virginia and neighboring Maryland had at one time been held in bondage by their own choosing.

A large group of America's first citizens did not voluntarily choose to come to the new country, but British policies of the day were geared toward shipping "undesirables" of any type out of the mother country and into the colonies.

Prostitutes and women from prison workhouses were forcibly transported to the New World, either as servants or as wives badly needed on the male-oriented frontier. Convicted criminals, debtors, and foreign soldiers captured by British armies were coerced aboard westbound ships and sold into virtual slavery in the colonies. This was considered the ultimate punishment for at least one felon; given his choice of life in America or death, he chose to be hanged. This large influx of felons did not mean that the colonies were suddenly flooded with hordes of convicted murderers, for at the time more than three hundred crimes, including the theft of a single shilling, were punishable by death. Orphans, or simply children walking the streets of London, were kidnapped by professional "spirits," who specialized in providing cheap child labor for the colonial market.

Black slaves were the largest group held in involuntary bondage. The first blacks brought by Engish settlers to America came under a type of limited indenture that lasted a specific period of time after which freedom was given. During the mid-seventeenth century, however, bondage for life became popular and soon slavery became a formal institution.

By 1760, slaves outnumbered whites two to one in South Carolina, were equal in number in Virginia, and on the eve of the Revolutionary War composed one-quarter of the population in the thirteen colonies.

In some areas, Indians were also taken as slaves, on an equal footing with

Tattooed Indians welcome Pilgrims to a feast. Woodcut, c. 1700. *Photo courtesy Library of Congress.*

blacks. But most of the colonies' red men were free to roam the woods, subsisting only by their own hand. Many tribes shared their centuries-old recipes with the new pioneers and, as a result, left a permanent mark on American cooking habits. Without the almost constant charity of friendly Indians who provided food to starving settlers, thousands of the first colonists would not have survived.

Although a few imported spices or preservatives were occasionally available to the poorer colonists, most lived completely on nature's crops, or in the case of slaves upon handout rations from their owners. Small game, seasonal vegetables, wild berries, and large amounts of cornmeal formed the diet of the masses. Food stored in the backwoods cabin or slave shanty was like a calendar of seasons, reflecting what was available from nature rather than what was available on the money market.

Regional differences also contributed to the great diversity in eating habits.

The elaborate but sedate feasts infrequently given in puritan New England could not approach the almost continual celebrations that characterized life in the South. In Maryland, Virginia, the Carolinas, and Georgia, every important holiday, and some not so important, was considered due cause for extravagant dining and dancing at all levels of society.

Warmer climates in these lower colonies also meant longer seasons for fresh vegetables and fruits. Thus, the diets of southern settlers included fewer pickled and preserved dishes than were necessary in the colder northern regions where growing periods were shorter and winters were longer. In addition, the great number of slave cooks in the South injected an African influence in cooking that was seen only occasionally north of the Mason-Dixon line.

Great differences are recorded not only from North to South, but also from the eastern seacoast towns to the western frontier settlements. The life of the harried pioneer wife in Kentucky was not conducive to the same type of cooking as that done by the spouse of a seaman in cosmopolitan Annapolis, although their economic conditions may have been identical.

In larger eastern towns, street vendors, taverns, inns, and dockside shops sold foodstuffs of a wide variety, thus permitting most urban families to maintain only a small garden plot capable of sustaining the family in brief times of hardship.

The large number of rural and western settlers, however, had little access to commercial stores, and subsisted on homegrown staples supplemented by their own hunting bag. These country settlers by far outnumbered city dwellers, for immediately prior to the 1776 rebellion, an estimated nine-tenths of the colonial population resided on farmlands.

But perhaps the greatest influence on American cooking was ethnic.

Most early settlers were first- or second-generation immigrants who lived in rurally isolated settlements primarily composed of other immigrants from the same country. Exchanges of recipes or cooking ideas with other nationalities were severely hindered by this physical separation. Language was also a barrier to the establishment of a single ''American way'' of cooking, for even in larger urban areas, English was not universally spoken.

Eating habits of the old countries did not die quickly, for America was a hodgepodge of various national customs. For example, in 1776 more than 40 percent of the white colonials were non-English.

The major groups included the German and Dutch, with their love of pickled vegetables and sausages; the French, and their generous hand with wines; and the Irish, Scotch, and Welsh, who contributed numerous puddings and stews. Smaller settlements of Spaniards, Swiss, Swedes, and Finns also added their culinary arts to the country's melting pot of cooking habits.

In everyday life, economic, geographical, and ethnic differences determined not only what types of food the New World pioneer would eat, but when he would eat, in what amount, and how the food would be prepared. This diversity of cooking habits among the colonies' early settlers was matched only by the abundant variety of foodstuffs in America's native lands.

The Residence of David Twining, 1787, by Edward Hicks. American, oil on canvas, c. 1846. Courtesy Abby Aldrich Rockefeller Folk Art Collection, Williamsburg, Virginia.

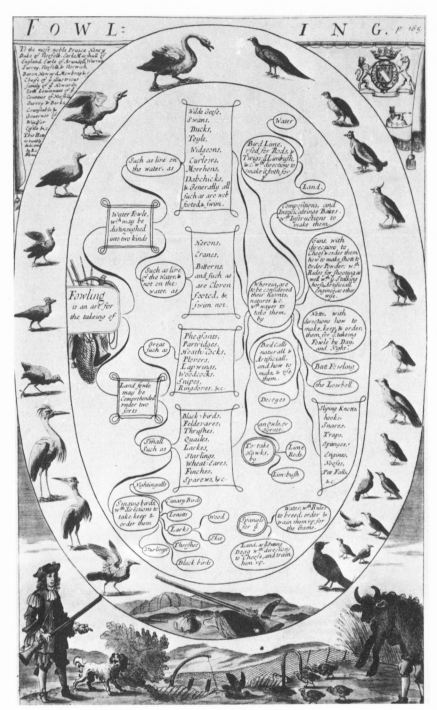

Fowling. Black and white etching, c. 1686–1710. *Courtesy Colonial Williamsburg, Williamsburg, Virginia.*

Cooking in the Home

The earliest settlers were poorly equipped, for space limitations on immigrant ships prohibited the transportation of many useful implements. One list distributed to prospective colonizers living in England suggested that only basic food rations and cooking utensils should be packed for the journey and first year's survival. Among the items included were:

In Vitals

For one man for one yeere:

Eight bushells of meale	Two gallons of vinegar
Two bushells of oatmeale	One gallon of aquavitae
One bushell of pease	One bushell of Bay salt
One gallon of oyle	Sugar, Spices and Fruit

Cooking Utensils

For six persons:

One iron pot	Two skillets
One iron kettle	One Spit
One large frying pan	Platters, dishes and spoones of wood
One gridiron	

Shipboard Provisions

Fine wheate flour
Claret wine burnt
Canary sacke
Conserves
Marmalades
Dried Neats tongue
Some weathersheepe
Leggs of Mutton,
  minced and stewed
  and close packed up
  in tried Sewet or
  butter in earthen pots

Suckets
Spices
Salat oyle
Prunes to stew
Live poultry
Gammons of Bacon
Juyce of Limons

Rice
Butter
Holland Cheese or old
  Chesire
Porke
Beefe packed up in
  Vinegar

To Trade

Wine, sugar, prunes, raisins, currance, honey, spice and grocery wares to trade for cattel, hogges, poultry and corne.

For the House

Mault for beere
Hogshead of Beefe or Porke
Two or three firkins of butter

A hundred or two old cheeses
A Gallon of Honey
Pookes for Rennet to make Cheese

For the Farm

Seede Wheate
Rie
Oates
Barley

Kernalls of Peares and Apples for
  making Cider and Perry
Stones and Seeds of all fruits, roots
  and herbs desireth to have

Implements for creating meals did not make pioneer woman's job easier, for most were homemade items that differed little from those used during the Middle Ages. Her real work began after the day's dinner had been either shot, caught, picked, or ground, and the heavy wooden logs had been chopped to feed the daylong cooking fire. But the most striking difference between food preparation today and that in the colonial era was the actual means by which food was cooked. For nearly ten generations before the first American cook-stove was cast in 1765, pioneer women depended upon the open hearth.

The fireplace was undoubtedly the center of attention and survival in early one-room cabins, for it provided not only a method of food preparation, but also the major source of both heat and light.

Construction of the fireplace and chimney differed in various sections of the country, but originally most northern settlers favored building with field-stones held together by mud or a rude oyster shell mortar. In the South, bricks made from local clay were most widely used. In primitive backwoods settlements of temporary dwellings, green wood was occasionally chosen for sections of the chimney, but this practice was eliminated gradually because of the great danger of accidental fire. As villages became more densely populated, the possibility increased that a fire spreading from house to house could wipe out an entire village. Some areas outlawed wooden accessories for chimneys and appointed inspectors to ensure the regulations were obeyed.

As the new arrivals to the colonies prospered and expanded their dwellings to more than a single room, fireplaces were sometimes placed inside the dwelling on a central wall. In this manner, a single chimney would provide flues for openings in two different rooms. On one side of the chimney was usually a large cooking fireplace opening into the kitchen, while on the other was a more moderate sized hearth, usually serving the parlor.

With this system, heat could be distributed more effectively throughout the house and the necessity of erecting two chimneys was eliminated. But because of the hazard of an accidental blaze spreading through the common wall and destroying the house, most settlers continued to place their fireplaces on an outside wall.

In the great mansions of the period, three or four separate chimneys were commonplace and necessary to make the many rooms bearable during cold winter nights. Nomini Hall, the residence of Virginia's Robert Carter, was heated by twenty-eight fireplaces, which required three full oxcarts of wood each day. Few citizens could match Carter's wealth, however, for his landhold-ings alone covered more than seventy thousand acres in the fertile tidewater area.

Wealthy plantation owners in the South constructed separate buildings for cooking, far away from the main house. This safer practice eliminated both cooking odors and oppressive heat from the living quarters, but made it

The Plantation. Artist unknown. American, oil on wood, c. 1825. *Courtesy The Metropolitan Museum of Art, gift of Edgar William and Bernice Chrysler Garbisch, 1963.*

very difficult to serve a hot meal. As a result, small warming pantries were added to the great houses to assure that dishes would be hot when served.

On many plantations, it was also fashionable to maintain other small out-buildings, each dealing with a particular aspect of food preparation. Among the most common were individual structures for slaughtering, smoking, bak-ing, food storage, and dairying. The cold northern winters that snowbound many houses, and the lack of a large slave class to carry the food, made the practice of separate cooking facilities unusual north of Pennsylvania.

Fireplace openings ranged from about four feet to more than ten feet in width, and in some cases they were as high as the kitchen ceiling. Generally, fireplaces in southern homes tended to be larger, but the recess in the house of New York Quaker John Bowne was large enough to roast an entire ox. Thick metal plates called ironbacks were usually placed at the rear of the opening. The idea was that the plates would reflect both heat and light into the entire room.

The hearth, which served as a food-warming area, was most often made from the same material as the chimney and reached several feet into the room. The purpose of this extended hearth was to prevent sparks and hot grease from landing on the wooden floor or rag rugs.

Bricks or stones, which formed the upper front wall, were supported by a thick wooden or stone beam called a mantel tree. The family's long gun and powder horn were usually hung from the mantel in quick readiness in case of an attack from Indians, wild animals, or unfriendly neighbors. Cooking utensils and herbs were also placed on this timber in near reach of the cook. In some Dutch areas, the stones above the mantel were draped with a ruffled cloth hood called a pawn. This item was for purely decorative purposes, rather than of any functional value, just as was the elaborate carving that was sometimes done on the mantel beam. Gaily painted tiles also helped to enliven the drab stone facade, but these imported items were used for the most part, by higher income families who could afford the costly prices.

Foot-wide rock ledges were sometimes built into the sides of the vast fireplaces and served literally as fireside chairs on which members of the family could warm themselves. Rank had its privileges in colonial days, for these seats were, by custom, places of honor reserved for guests or adult members of the family.

The fireplace or clavelpiece, was constructed specifically to provide the best possible arrangement for cooking. On each side of the fireplace, just

A cat painted on six delft tiles. Composite pictures such as this were often used to decorate colonial fireplaces. *Courtesy The Shelburne Museum, Inc., Shelburne, Vermont.*

below mantel level, were two small ledges on which rested a round rod. From this sturdy lug pole, pots were hung for cooking. In poorer homes lug poles, also called backbars, were made from green wood, which was wetted periodically or completely replaced to retard burning.

A lug pole that burned through at an inopportune time meant that the dinner pot dropped directly into the fire, not only spoiling the meal but possibly severely burning any bystanders. As families became more affluent, iron poles were substituted for the wood, thus eliminating the danger of injury from scalding.

Pots that hung from the lug pole were raised or lowered above the fire by means of S-shaped hooks, adjustable ratchets, trammels, hakes, or chains. By adjusting the height of her pot from the fire, the housewife could regulate the speed of cooking much like the burners of present-day ranges. A pot hung on the shortest hook was highest from the fire and produced a slow simmering. A low-hung pot on a longer ratchet was needed to produce a fast or rolling boil.

Instead of a lug pole, swinging metal cranes connected to hinges built into the sides of the fireplace supported the cooking pots of most southern families. The crane arrangement became popular in the North sometime during the eighteenth century. In addition to eliminating the danger of scalding caused by burnt-through lug poles, cranes rotated well out onto the hearth area. Thus, these safer attachments allowed the cook to stir the pot or add ingredients well away from the flames.

Baking was done in a small enclosed compartment built into the chimney next to the open hearth. The door to this recess opened either into the room or directly into the fireplace. Ovens facing into the fire naturally made it difficult to bake and cook on the hearth at the same time, for the chef was forced to walk inside the fireplace opening to place food in the bake oven. Burned clothing was probably not unusual, particularly since early American women cooked while wearing long skirts, which easily picked up scattered sparks. As a result, oven

Wrought-iron trammel pot hook with a typical chiseled decoration. American, eighteenth century. Courtesy National Gallery of Art, Index of American Design.

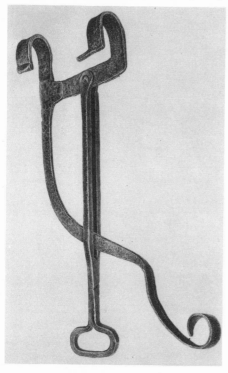

Iron kettle tilter. American, seventeenth or eighteenth century. Courtesy National Gallery of Art, Index of American Design.

doors that opened into the fireplace were gradually eliminated in favor of those that faced into the room.

Baking was probably done only once or twice a week, for it involved elaborate preparations. First, a roaring fire was built inside the bake oven and allowed to burn for several hours so that the walls were thoroughly heated. Next the burning coals were swept from the area and the baked goods were placed inside on leaves or on tin sheets by using a long-handled peel. Finally, the oven door was sealed tight with clay to prevent heat from escaping. Most baking required many hours, and such items as breads were often left overnight to complete cooking. Like lug poles, oven doors were made originally of wood, but later were replaced by iron as iron products became more widely available.

More elaborate chimneys included not only flues for the open hearth and bake oven, but also for other special compartments built into the fireplace area.

An Indian method for boiling corn in earthen pots, by John White. English, watercolor, c. 1577–1590. *Courtesy Trustees of The British Museum.*

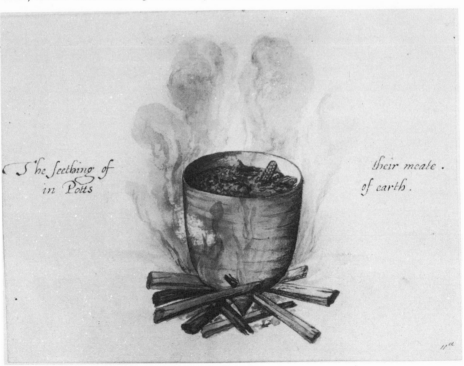

Smoke ovens for preparing hams and bacon inside the house, and ash ovens that provided facilities for slow roasting of large cuts of meat, were often added to the basic fireplace structure.

Despite elaborate chimney systems for numerous types of ovens, baking never became the most common method of cooking. Hashes, ragouts, and traditional boiled dinners that could be slowly stewed were undoubtedly the most widely accepted dishes, primarily because of their relative ease of preparation.

Cooking was simply another chore for the early housewife who had scores of other daily tasks to complete while dinner was in the making. Combinations of chopped meat and vegetables could simmer unattended in the pot for several hours, during which the settler woman attended to her other jobs.

Slow boiling was also ideal for cooking porridges, which were often mixed after supper and allowed to cook at low temperatures throughout the night. Many wild meats, which tended to be tough, also needed a long period of cooking or stewing in order to make them edible.

Roasting was a third method of prerevolutionary cooking, but one usually reserved for cuts of domestic stock or the most tender sections of game animals.

Andirons, or firedogs, were equipped with special notches for supporting the spit on which meats were skewered for roasting. If andirons were lacking, the meat was wrapped in a rope sling and hung from the lug pole. Using either method, the meat was turned periodically to assure even cooking, and a pan was placed just below the roast to catch the drippings for use in basting or in flavoring other dishes.

Children were often assigned the job of turning the spit, but more elaborate roasting mechanisms were devised as the country became more advanced technologically. Special automatic jacks or clock-driven mechanisms with weights and pulleys were used. The most complicated may have been a series of wheels that were connected to the spit and powered by a dog walking on a treadmill. Another model, called a smokejack, looked and worked like a miniature windmill turned by drafts of hot air from the fireplace.

Late in the seventeenth century, less cumbersome methods of roasting were introduced in America. Many homes used portable metal ovens called roasting kitchens. These ovens were shaped like rectangular boxes, but were open on the side that was placed before the fire. Smaller versions of this apparatus, known as rabbit roasters, were used in preparing any small game or bird.

Oversized iron or bell-metal pots with tight-fitting lids were also developed for roasting. These containers, placed inside the fireplace and covered with hot coals, were also used in baking. Because of their popularity in the middle colonies, the name Dutch oven was applied to this covered container.

Frying or poaching were probably not daily cooking techniques in most homes. A primary reason was the basic dangerous nature of open hearth

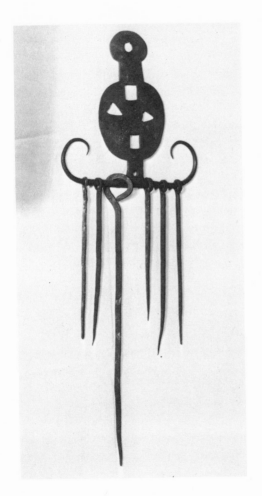

Wrought-iron skewers and holder used as accessories for a fireplace spit. American, eighteenth century. *Courtesy National Gallery of Art, Index of American Design.*

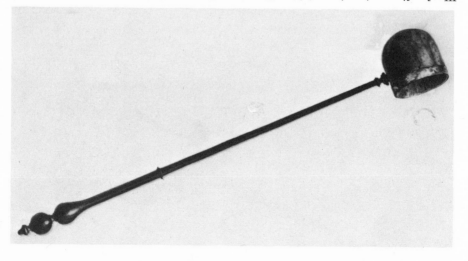

Wooden dipper. American, eighteenth century. *Courtesy National Gallery of Art, Index of American Design.*

cooking. Skillets with handles of up to three feet in length were needed to reach into the fire if the housewife was to stand in a safe position on the hearth. Frying pans could be set on long-legged trivets, but the action of turning the food without upsetting the skillet required a steady hand. This problem was solved in some degree by the manufacture of spiders, special skillets with legs attached to the bottom of the pan and specifically used for frying over an open fire.

Splattering fat or flammable grease into the fire was an additional hazard in frying, as were the long-handled wooden spoons or turning spatulas that could catch fire at any moment. Finally, frying required much closer attention than other cooking methods, a distinct drawback for the harried colonial cook.

Long before white men arrived with their metal pots and pans, eastern Indians who rarely ate raw food of any type had developed elaborate systems of cooking.

Cakes, breads and ears of corn were wrapped in protective layers of leaves and then placed among the warm ashes to be roasted. Meats were skewered on sharp sticks and held above the fire, just as today's campers toast marshmallows or hot dogs. Broiling large sections of meats or fish was done on a wooden platform constructed above the campfire.

Copper sauce pot. American, seventeenth century. *Courtesy National Gallery of Art, Index of American Design.*

Boiling was common to all eastern tribes and was the squaw's version of stewing. Direct fire boiling was done in stone or clay containers set into the coals. Several tribes also used stone boiling, whereby rocks were heated in the campfire and then thrown into clay pots filled with water and food. As the rocks cooled, they were removed and more hot stones thrown in.

Boiling was used for preparing all types of Indian dishes, including one special multicourse meal. First, various joints of game were boiled until tender, removed, and eaten. The bones were then thrown back into the pot with herbs and finally thickened with powdered maize to produce a second course of thick soup.

Braves on the trail used deer hides or bark-lined pouches as boiling containers, but these tended to burn through on the bottom after being used several times and were probably not used in permanent villages.

Baking was done in earth ovens, a practice that has been continued by modern picnickers on clambakes. First, a hole was dug into the ground and partially filled with hot coals. The food, wrapped in leaves, was placed on top of the coals and the pit refilled with a mixture of dirt and more hot coals.

Water poured over the mound permitted steam to form inside and helped to soften the food as it cooked. The earth ovens were then left undisturbed for several hours or days, depending upon the type of food that was being cooked. Coastal Indians built similar ovens aboveground and added seaweed to the dirt to build up steam.

Cooking was a daylong activity for Indian women, for most tribes ate almost continuously throughout the day. Members of certain North Carolina tribes were said to arise even at midnight for a mid-sleep snack to tide them through until morning.

Whether the pioneer woman baked her corn bread Indian fashion or European style, or cooked her meats in an open fire or in an imported roaster, certain basic utensils were required to get the job done. In some communities artisans produced a small number of utensils for

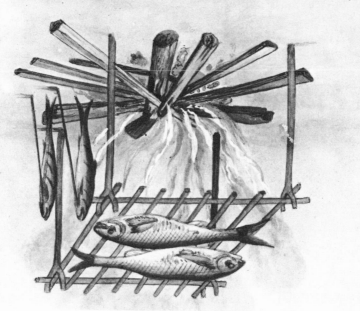

Fish cooking Indian-style on a wood platform, English watercolor by John White, c. 1577–1590. Photo courtesy Library of Congress.

Sh1ive fitting at meate

An Indian dinner of meat and maize, by John White. English, watercolor, c. 1577–1590. *Photo courtesy Library of Congress.*

sale. In Cornhill, Massachusetts, Mary Jackson both sold and manufactured kettles, pots, and pans. But, cooking aids for most colonists were homemade until the widespread introduction of imported English products and the advent of traveling peddlers. As a result of this reliance on home improvisation, utensils varied in shape and size from family to family. Collectors of early Americana are well familiar with the many types of early toasters, colanders, sifters, beaters, strainers, and skimmers.

Although food was abundant in the colonies, money was not and many women used their few cooking utensils to serve many functions. A paddle used to stir porridge in the morning could be used to make soap in the evening. Molds were handy not only for making puddings, but for breads, butter, and cheeses. Rolling pins were used not only for rolling pastry dough, but also for beating the toughness out of freshly killed game.

Because most vegetables and meats were simply prepared, the most elaborate utensils were connected with the production of pastries and desserts. Pie crimpers, a contraption resembling a lollypop with a serrated edge, were used to press together upper and lower crusts of pies. Pastry jiggers were used to give a decorative edge to cookies. Wooden or pierced tin sieves, used to strain berry or nut preserves, doubled as colanders.

Most utensils were made of wood, iron, or bell metal, although during the late seventeenth century, brass and copper made inroads into the markets of seacoast towns and urban areas. One particularly popular metal was called latten and was produced as a brass alloy. Much of the tin cooking ware in use during the period was not the light material of modern production. Rather, it was sheet iron, plated with tin and, therefore, quite heavy to handle. Both homemade and imported items did have certain similarities that distinguish them from modern products. Generally, all pots used for cooking on the floor of the fireplace had long legs to raise them above the direct flames. Frying pans, ladles, toasters, and waffle irons were manufactured with

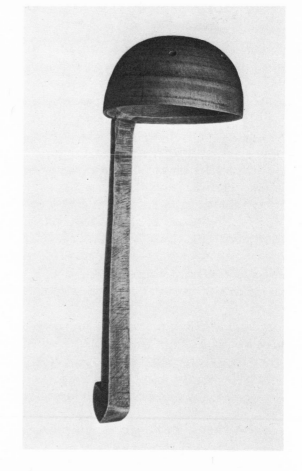

Wooden strainer also used for skimming and stirring food. American, seventeenth century. *Courtesy National Gallery of Art, Index of American Design.*

Iron trivet used for warming foods on the hearth. American, seventeenth century. *Courtesy National Gallery of Art, Index of American Design.*

long handles so they could be shaken or held for cooking while the chef stood far back on the hearth.

Food-warming or cooking, which required very low heat, was done on long-legged trivets that sat upon the hearth or on a metal-warming shelf that could be placed on the andirons. Also necessary in the early American kitchen were weighing scales, for no standard measures existed and most recipes were prepared according to the weight of the ingredients. Bellows to fan the fire-place flames were also a necessity.

Storage of food was a problem in those days, before handy glass or plastic food containers. Baskets woven from pine needles, willow, cornhusks, or reeds were made for keeping dry staples, such as cheese and corn.

Colonists may have sunk the baskets into the ground Indian fashion to keep them cool in hot weather. This practice was well known to early settlers, for one of the first discoveries of Plymouth's Pilgrims was the location of an Indian tribe's corn supply, buried for winter storage in underground baskets. The Pilgrims promptly dug up this buried treasure and stole the corn.

Pottery and stoneware crocks were invaluable for those who could afford their price and were particularly needed for the storage of liquids, such as vinegars, molasses, beverages, and pickles or preserves. Homemade earthen-ware pots were probably the most widely used storage crocks.

Meats and grain sacks were hung from the rafters or stored in the attic to minimize damage from water or field rodents. In some houses, small game was hung from a special iron chandelier with upturned spikes instead of candle

Indians taking their crops to the public granary, 1564. Engraving after Frenchman Jacques Le Moyne de Morgues, 1591. *Photo courtesy Library of Congress.*

Wooden triangle water bag probably made by a professional American artisan in the eighteenth century. *Courtesy National Gallery of Art, Index of American Design.*

holders. The idea was to both bleed the meat and keep it out of the reach of the family's dogs. Similar contraptions called Dutch crowns were used to suspend meat while it was being smoked.

Of prime importance to every family were containers for various medicinal brews prepared by the housewife from herbs and plants. Because even the most elementary dietary rules were unknown, gout, distemper, and other digestive ills were painfully common. The pioneer housewife also served as an amateur pharmacist, dispensing her specially concocted home remedies for the sicknesses that constantly afflicted her family.

With the rise of great personal fortunes during the late seventeenth century, many colonial women left the preparation and cleanup of meals to slave cooks and kitchen helpers. This practice was not confined to the South,

Cedar pail, American, eighteenth century. *Courtesy National Gallery of Art, Index of American Design.*

but was also common in northern areas where slavery was less widespread but not unusual.

The black cook began planning for dinner early in the day as soon as the first fires were built by the slave children. Only after the main meal's meats, vegetables, and pastries were set on the fire to cook, did she begin preparation of breakfast.

One practice, noted by ex-colonial slave Gustavus Vassa, makes the present-day chef wonder how these black cooks were able to produce the superb dishes for which they were noted.

In his journal, Vassa records his surprise at discovering a Virginia slave cook busily at her work in the kitchen, but wearing a heavy iron muzzle around her head and mouth. The purpose of this contraption was to prohibit slaves from eating or drinking the master's food while it was being prepared.

This invention may have helped to conserve the food supply of the wealthy owner, particularly when slaves were usually given minimum rations, but it could not have been too successful in promoting properly seasoned dishes. Of course, food sampling may have been done by the mistress of the house, who also planned the day's menu and oversaw its preparation.

While slave cooks eased the labor of southern white women, their presence in the kitchen presented a danger, real or imagined, for the health of the owner. Among the most severe penalties in colonial slave codes were those for poisoning. Then, as today, the wild plants of the forest yielded not only succulent greens but deadly herbs. Laws prescribing death by tortuous methods were attempts to prevent the dissatisfied slave cook from disposing of her owner and his family with one fell swoop.

Because teaching slaves to read or write was a severe offense in most areas, there are no accurate records of recipes originated by slave cooks. The amounts and ingredients used in dishes were either memorized and passed down through generations of blacks, or were read to the slaves by the mistress of the house, if she herself could read.

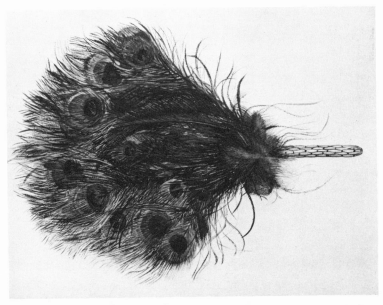

Peacock feather fan with a woven quill handle. American, made before 1860. *Courtesy National Gallery of Art, Index of American Design.*

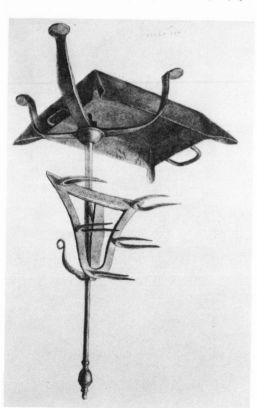

Roasting or meat toaster, with dripping pan. American, eighteenth century. *Courtesy National Gallery of Art, Index of American Design.*

Mrs. Thomas Jefferson was one of the fortunate female members of society who was educated, and a former slave of the family recalled in later years that Mrs. Jefferson read long recipes to her cooks.

Wealthy women occasionally prepared food themselves, but usually only in times when the demand was great, such as for balls and other celebrations. Cooking was limited to dainties, such as cakes and pastries, rather than to heavy work, such as turning a spit or roasting a beef carcass.

Much of the other activity connected with food preparation was left to black workers in slaveholding families. On large plantations, kitchen helpers may also have helped to churn butter, chop wood, brew spirits, tend the smokehouse, and slaughter meats. They also traditionally carried food from the cookhouse and served at meals. Perhaps the ultimate in specialization was during the summer in the South where blacks stood at the planter's dinner table to brush away flies with a peacock fan.

On small farms, slaves were probably relegated to fieldwork only, and most food-related activities were performed by the owner's wife, just as in poor families and nonslaveholding communities.

Iron back for fireplace. American, dated 1763 and inscribed *Cole·Brook·Dale· Furnace. Courtesy National Gallery of Art, Index of American Design.*

Eating in the Home

A separate room for cooking, away from sleeping or living areas, did not become common until many years after the colonies were settled, and until the eighteenth century was not found in the homes of most families.

Kitchens, because of their multipurpose use of sleeping, eating, and cook-ing, were called halls or common rooms. Most were bare by today's standards of furnishing and small in size. Furniture-making was a time-consuming process and usually was performed by the master of the house in his leisure moments, which were few. Most of the colonial husbandman's time was allocated to more important tasks of everyday survival such as hunting and farming.

The dining table, or board, in the standard cabin for poorer families was made from roughhewn timbers or from sturdy packing boxes used in trans-atlantic shipping. In middle-class homes, tables may have been more stylish and purchased from a local cabinetmaker for cash or in exchange for foodstuffs grown by the buyer's family. Elegant homes of the period were furnished lavishly with the finest products of English or colonial craftsmen.

The use of chairs in upper- and middle-class homes was probably common and similar to current practices. In poorer dwellings, easy to construct benches were most favored. Such families may have owned one chair, which was re-served for the man of the house to use not only at the table but at any time of day. The lack of chairs did not affect eating habits, for young children traditionally ate their meals while standing. Young people usually took their places behind the adults who were seated at the table; sometimes the children stood at a smaller side table used also for food preparation.

Even the adult members of frontier families were accustomed to standing while having their breakfast cider and porridge, and other meals in these same communities were not known as intimate family gatherings. Many of these settlers simply ate alone, whenever they were hungry or tired, helping themselves to the contents of the stewpot that was constantly simmering on the fire.

In more populated areas, the day began with a mug of some alcoholic drink taken immediately after rising. A typical breakfast in New England featured cornmeal mush and molasses, with cider or beer. Milk was usually reserved for the babies of the family, or on special occasions for cooking. Tea,

The Dinner, by W. Dickinson. English, hand-colored engraving, 1794. *Courtesy Colonial Williamsburg, Williamsburg, Virginia.*

coffee, bread, cold meats, and fruit pies became popular in northern areas as early morning items when food became more plentiful.

Other settlers, particularly those in the South, ate more heartily and added cheese, meat pasties, fruits, and eggs to their basic breakfast of gruel. Scrapple, a blend of cornmeal and headcheese, was standard breakfast fare in the middle colonies where the morning meal was also quite heavy.

Holders of large, landed plantations traditionally delayed breakfast until midmorning, after the daily inspection of farm work was completed. In many areas, the planter was eating his first meal of the day at the same time that farm families who had begun work before dawn sat down to rest at their dinner. Midday dinner was customarily the largest meal and featured the most elaborately prepared dishes, many of which had been cooking since dawn. Supper came several hours later, was usually brief, and consisted of leftovers from dinner or of gruel. Supper for the small farmer could be at three in the afternoon, but the plantation owner usually did not eat until nine in the evening. Some families eliminated the supper meal entirely and existed only on early morning breakfast and midafternoon dinner.

Still another schedule existed for the many Americans who were not free to choose the time to eat. Field slaves, who began working soon after the first light, probably did not receive their breakfast until two or three hours later. This first meal and the larger dinner meal, which was served about noon, were prepared in great quantities in a central slave kitchen. Food was brought to the fields in large buckets and ladled into clay dishes or onto boards. Small children, who were sent to a communal nursery while their parents toiled, were also fed en masse.

On large plantations, the final meal of the day was prepared in individual slave quarters by the women of the cabin, using food received as part of the weekly rations. On smaller farms and on tobacco plantations where slave work continued at night in the stacking sheds, this supper meal may also have been prepared in the central kitchen.

In urban areas and in the North, slaves and free black servants may have eaten food similar to that of the owner's family, but their meals were often taken in the kitchen or in their separate quarters. There is some evidence that in middle-class families in the North, slaves may have eaten at the table with their masters, an astounding difference from the situation of their brothers in the South.

Ensign Thomas Hughes, a British officer captured during the Revolution at the Battle of Ticonderoga, but paroled on good behavior, left a complete record of the early eating habits of middle-class America. Hughes paid two silver dollars a week for room and board in a private household in Pepperell, Massachusetts, and his good-natured amazement at colonial customs is evident in his diary. He was particularly astonished at the democratic customs of America, for he wrote:

We have but one room to eat and sit in, which is common with all the family, master, mistress, and servant, and what to call it, I know not, as it serves for parlour, kitchen and workroom. About 9 o'clock, Lt. Brown (who lives with me) and myself breakfast, but they all wonder how we can sleep so long. Our breakfast is bread and milk, or boil'd Indian corn with butter and treacle spread over it . . .

About 12 o'clock the whole family collects for dinner, which soon after smokes upon the board; and whilst it is cooling, Father shuts his eyes, mutters an unintelligible monstrous long grace and down we all sit with no other distinction, but Brown and me getting pewter plates—whereas the others have wooden platters. Our food is fat salt pork and sauce (the name they give to roots and greens) . . .

The dinners are upon that free and easy mode, that neither gentleman or lady use any ceremony—all hands in the dish at once—which gives many pretty opportunities for laughter, as two or three of us often catch hold of the same piece . . .

About 8 o'clock, we get bread and milk for supper . . . Our room is not the worst for being a repository of fruit and nuts, as we generally make an attack on the apples before we get up a morn. If this is the kind of life the poets say so much of, and call Rural Happiness, I wish to my soul that they were here, and I in London.

One month later Hughes gained at least part of his wish for he was no longer living with the family in Pepperell. The young officer's parole was revoked after he and several British comrades attended a boisterous party at a local inn where several became "mellow" and spoke disrespectfully of Congress.

Hughes was politely offered his choice of jail in either Cambridge or Concord, and choosing Cambridge, was delivered to the turnkey with orders to be treated kindly.

In homes poorer than the Pepperell family, settlers ate directly from the cooking pot, which was brought from the fire and placed in the center of the table along with a bowl of coarse salt. However, most Americans ladled their food from the kettle onto wooden plates called trenchers. These were simply made from a flat board that had been whittled or scooped out in the center to form a hollow depression or trench.

Trenchers and other eating woodenware were called treen and today are highly valued relics of colonial times. Most of these early crude items were homemade, but by the mid-eighteenth century, merchants in New Hampshire and Vermont commercially produced more elaborate wooden plates, bowls, and assorted utensils.

One trencher was often used by two diners, and in many areas courting couples seen eating from the same trencher were considered automatically engaged to be married. In some homes, individual trenchers were unknown, and settlers ate from shallow impressions that had been scooped directly out of the tabletop.

Eating utensils were also primitive. Many used their fingers to eat whole foods, while soups were consumed using a homemade wooden spoon, hollowed-out gourd, or seashell. This practice resulted in any type of stew being nicknamed spoon meat. During the progression of colonial settlement, spoons changed radically in shape. The first products were short-handled affairs, with almost round bowls that were extremely shallow. As time passed, the handles became longer and thinner, while the bowl became more oval and deeper. Designs began to appear on the tips of the handles, an indication that the people and the country were becoming more affluent and could turn their attention away from the purely functional to the decorative.

Pewter and silver spoons gained popularity in wealthy circles during the seventeenth century, but it was not until the mid-eighteenth century that a majority of the people ate with knives and forks. Before this time, meat was carved with a hunting knife, and forks, when available, were two-tined affairs used primarily to hold a roast of meat for slicing. These early implements were usually wood or bone handled, with the more elaborate ivory handles coming into vogue during the later period.

Both knives and forks were highly valued and made a gift of significance. Boston magistrate Samuel Sewall recorded in his diary a present especially chosen for his lady friend Mrs. Denison. ''I give her two Cases with a knife and fork in each,'' he proudly wrote, adding that a pound of raisins was also included. Sewall, one of the judges at the Salem witch trials and the only one to recant later, seemed to frequently time his visits to friends at the dinner hour. Guests at meals customarily arrived with their own spoons and knives, not so much as a matter of courtesy, but out of necessity. In most homes, eating utensils were available only for members of the immediate family. A particularly practical solution to the tableware problem was a device known

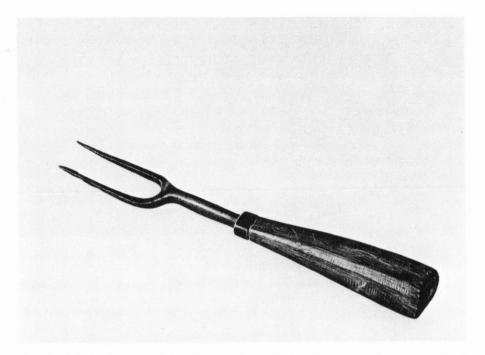

Two-tined fork with wooden handle. American, eighteenth century. *Courtesy National Gallery of Art, Index of American Design.*

as the sucket spoon. This ingenious development featured a two-pronged fork at one end and a spoon on the other. Folding utensils were also popular, particularly for traveling.

Until French customs concerning manners became influential in America around 1800, all dishes were placed on the table and passed from person to person. Even in the wealthiest homes servants did not carry food directly to the diners, except in those aristocratic families with French connections.

Large napkins were used to protect the clothing at almost all levels of society. These were greatly needed, for eating with fingers or with a crude spoon was a greasy proposition and usually spelled disaster to colonial clothing. Great pieces of cloth were usually tied around the diner's neck and fell well into his lap.

Tablecloths, though fashionable in England, were used rarely in the early colonies, where citizens of all economic groups placed their dishes directly on bare table-boards. As citizens grew wealthier and middle-class women gained more leisure time, cloths of fine damask were either imported or stitched up in the home. Rough homespun was the most popular choice of the average family. Mrs. Elizabeth Diggs of Virginia was a fancier of linens, for her 1699 estate inventory included 126 napkins and 60 tablecloths.

After meals, dishes were removed from the table in a large basket called a voider. Often water had to be carried long distances from streams and soap was usually precious so there was probably little elaborate dishwashing in most homes. Trenchers and spoons were simply wiped clean and stored for the next meal. In some villages such as Jamestown, ordinances prohibited dish-washing within a specified area around the town well or pump. These attempts at keeping the water supply sanitary resulted in housewives often lugging sixty pound iron pots far downstream to be cleaned. In homes where servants or slaves performed the clean-up tasks, more sanitary conditions may have existed than in the house of the folk family.

The rough American etiquette proved too much for Scottish-born Dr. Alexander Hamilton on his 1744 journey from Annapolis to Maine. Hamilton reported that he quickly lost his stomach for food while observing the family of a ferryman eating a meal. In his journal, Hamilton described the fish dinner of this simple family living on the banks of the Susquehanna River:

They had no cloth upon the table, and their mess was in a dirty, deep, wooden dish which they evacuated with their hands, cramming down skins, scales, and all. They used neither knife, fork, spoon, plate, or napkin because, I suppose, they had none to use.

Hamilton did share a cup of cider with the group and, with perhaps typical European chauvinism of the period, suggested that American culture was at a similar state to the barbaric days of his long forgotten ancestors:

I looked upon this as a picture of that primitive simplicity practiced by our forefathers long before the mechanic arts had supplied them with instruments for the luxury and elegance of life.

Liquids were first drunk from pottery or wooden pitchers called noggins, which were passed from mouth to mouth. A more personal vessel was the black-jack mug, a container made from boiled leather, sewn together in a beaker shape and rimmed with metal. As families became prosperous, they accumu-

Kettles such as this often weighed as much as sixty pounds when empty. American. *Courtesy National Gallery of Art, Index of American Design.*

lated individual steins made from pewter, silver, or china, and the communal drinking noggin was gradually discarded.

Families one step up the economic ladder from those who were solely dependent upon treen used pewter items such as plates, mugs, beakers, porringers, and spoons. Porringers came in all sizes and shapes and were used not only at breakfast but any time that a dish in liquid form was served. These popular items were common at American tables long after their use had been discontinued in England about 1750.

Wealthy colonists often took their savings of silver coins to artisans such as Paul Revere who melted down the metal tender and prepared eating utensils from the raw material. The resulting products were called coin silver. The

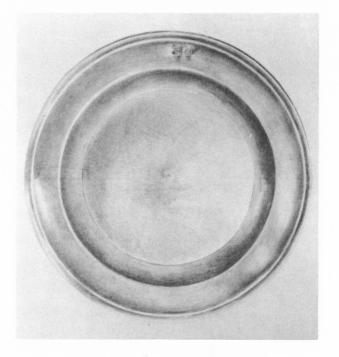

Pewter plate. American. Courtesy National Gallery of Art, Index of American Design.

Pewter mug. American. Courtesy National Gallery of Art, Index of American Design.

Pewter beaker. American. *Courtesy National Gallery of Art, Index of American Design.*

owner's initials were almost automatically engraved on the products to make them easily traceable in case of theft. Crests or specially designed seals also served as signatures of ownership similar to cattle brands.

America's long history of distinguished metal artisans stems from the early Jamestown settlement when two goldsmiths, two refiners, and a jeweler landed in 1608. These workers, sent to evaluate the supposed great hoards of riches anticipated by the English, ''never had occasion to exercise their craft,'' according to John Smith. Later, however, silversmiths thrived in Boston, Providence, New York, and Philadelphia, but their wares were produced for only a small group of select buyers.

Sheffield plate was also available as an imported item of lesser cost than pure or sterling silver. In this English-developed process, silver and copper are fused into a product which is heavier, cheaper, and more durable than solid silver pieces.

Plate was a term that was used not only for Sheffield products, or to describe a specifically shaped dish, but was applied to any item made from silver ore. Derived from the Spanish word plata, meaning silver, the term plate became popular during this time when much imported silver came from the Iberian peninsula.

Pewter basin. American. *Courtesy National Gallery of Art, Index of American Design.*

The fine silver candlesticks, teapots, coffee urns, two-handled caudle cups, chocolate pots, tankards, and beakers, which were so valued in wealthy homes, created problems for less fortunate settlers. Many British citizens who visited only the richest class of Americans returned to England convinced that more stringent taxes should be enacted on the colonies, where so many citizens dined in such a grand manner.

The wide use of costly metals in eating utensils did not come to great numbers of citizens until just prior to the Revolution. Their use was short-lived. During the war for independence, many cherished household items made from silver, pewter, and brass were melted down for use as bullet casings, or as currency to trade with European allies.

Fine imported china was available to accompany the silver possessions of the upper classes. By the eighteenth century, Dutch, English, and German manufacturers were all catering to customers in America. Perhaps of equal importance to the wealthy American were Chinese export items.

Great sets of made-to-order exportware were produced in China for the American market. The monogrammed and blue and white patterns were the most popular, but the discriminating buyer could receive almost any design he desired. A sketch of the desired pattern would be sent to the Orient where

Silver caudle cup, made by Joseph Goldthwarte. American, second quarter eighteenth century. *Courtesy National Gallery of Art, Index of American Design.*

it would be painted onto the appropriate dishes. Chinese craftsmen could rarely restrain themselves from painting into the design part of the world that they knew. The North Carolina planter, unpacking his new set of Chinese dishes, might find his plantation home faithfully reproduced, but located in a field of bamboo with a dragon or temple in the background.

Originally European sea captains used Chinese tableware as ballast to be sold for any small profit in their home port. The demand for fine Oriental goods soon became tremendous and firms began to set up hongs or offices in cities such as Canton. Here representatives oversaw the painting of designs, which would be pleasing to Western tastes.

Traders without large amounts of money to purchase the items bartered furs to the Chinese. Soon a more valuable and easily obtainable commodity was discovered—American ginseng, a favorite food of the great wild turkey.

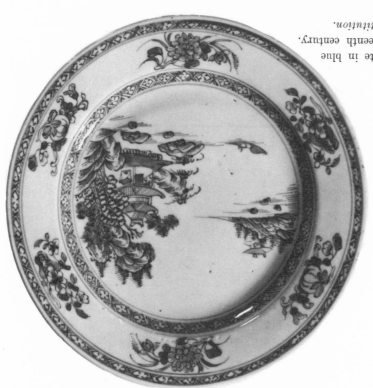

Oriental export porcelain plate in blue and white. Second half eighteenth century. *Courtesy The Smithsonian Institution.*

All early chinaware, whether produced in the Orient or in European factories, was hand painted, thus adding to the expense of manufacture and transportation. Prices for dishes were lowered following the invention of mechanical pattern stampers around 1750, thus enabling more colonists to purchase the items. But even these advances did not put china within the price range of most Americans in the middle classes.

Potters had begun producing rough earthenware and stoneware before the colonies were fifty years old. This crude, porous crockery was used primarily for food storage and everyday eating by those who wanted something better than treen without the cost of china. Pieces of gaily painted Italian and Spanish majolica were also used along with English or Dutch delft.

The great majority of settlers probably had little or no contact with any glass cooking or eating items during the first hundred years. The exception

The End of the Hunt. Artist unknown. American, oil on canvas, c. 1800. *Courtesy National Gallery of Art, Washington, D.C., gift of Edgar William and Bernice Chrysler Garbisch.*

may have been glass bottles from imported gin, wines, or brandies. Upper economic groups highly valued their glass property. Charles Carroll, a signer of the Declaration of Independence, went so far as to list his glass bottles in his will.

Indeed, the first industry set up in America may well have been a glassworks built in early Jamestown to produce windowpanes, bottles, and beads for trade with the Indians. The glass industry did not spread, for strict British regulations prohibiting glassworks were soon enacted to protect the manufacturers in England. A few works were set up despite the British ban, but glass products for the home were only occasional by-products from the main commercial business in windowpanes and bottles.

Whether the dishes were silver, pewter, or wood, and the food was simple wild game or the best domestic beef, a family's most treasured pieces were brought out on celebration days.

In the South, almost any diversion from ordinary daily activities prompted great feasts, complete with barrels of liquor, music, and dancing.

Most southerners celebrated the traditional English church festivals such as Christmas and Easter, and dinner after Sunday service was also an occasion for elaborate entertaining. Some groups recognized Guy Fawkes Day or Gunpowder Plot Day, along with commencement at the local school.

Fox-hunting meets, horse races, and other sporting events meant great daylong parties at the manor houses. Many toasts were drunk at balls commemorating the king's, queen's, and crown prince's birthdays, and visits by colonial governors or other high-ranking officials prompted elaborate banquets by the gentry.

On a lesser scale, average southern families entertained travelers with special social gatherings where the latest news of the outside world was passed along. Families pooled their food and drink in a communal celebration at some central spot and enjoyed cockfights, wrestling matches, and leaping contests. Housewives in Maryland and Virginia began preparing dishes days before the riotous community picnics, which were always held on Muster Day when the militia trained, twice a year, and at country fairs.

Christenings, marriages, and funerals also called for large amounts of food and drink. Participants often traveled long distances to attend these events, and their visits usually stretched into week-long sabbaticals at the host's home. Mourners at one funeral observance in York County, Virginia, in 1667, consumed twenty-two gallons of cider, twenty-four of beer, and five of brandy.

Because of the difficulties in bringing together friends and members of the family who lived many miles apart, multiple festivities would often be held during the day or week. Mourners at a funeral one afternoon could become celebrants at a marriage held the next morning, which in turn was followed by a baptism or christening.

Slaves were usually free from work about sixty days a year, including Sundays and holidays. While these were also designated as times to tend their private garden plots, periodic celebrations were allowed. Although laws prohibited slaves from leaving their homes without the consent of their owners, many blacks used the cover of darkness to visit friends at neighboring plantations for night parties. These gatherings were closely monitored, for many slaveholders viewed these afterwork gatherings not as relaxing parties, but as covers for clandestine plotting of slave revolts.

The middle colonists may have been a bit more subdued than their neighbors to the South. Among the particularly festive dates were New Year's, May Day, and Shrovetide, when special doughnut-like cookies, fastnachtskuchen, were baked.

The Old Plantation. Artist unknown. American, watercolor, c. 1777–1794. *Courtesy Abby Aldrich Rockefeller Folk Art Collection, Williamsburg, Virginia.*

Pinkster Day, which celebrated Pentecost, was widely recognized, particularly by slaves who marked the occasion by consuming great quantities of gingerbread and liquor. In New York, the festivities became so disruptive to the public that holiday celebrations were severely curtailed in order to preserve social harmony and sobriety.

One custom popular among New York's "Albanians" involved children's birthdays. Parents were expected to leave their houses on this day, while their children entertained friends with chocolate, preserved and dried fruits, cakes, cider, and syllabub. The festivities, which lasted until nine or ten at night, were discreetly chaperoned by a trusted servant.

In New England, harvests and sugaring offs were treated with as much gaiety as was allowable, and a major celebration was always planned in fall for Thanksgiving. Cornhuskings were attended by most members of the community with a special treat going to the man who found a red ear of corn. He was entitled to a kiss from the girl of his choice because of his good luck. This

High Life Below Stairs. English, mezzotint, 1770. *Courtesy Colonial Williamsburg, Williamsburg, Virginia.*

Judge Samuel Sewall, by John Smibert. American, oil on canvas, 1729. *Courtesy Museum of Fine Arts, Boston; bequest of William L. Barnard by exchange and the Emily L. Ainsley Fund.*

may have been a Puritan adaptation of a more spirited and less gentle Indian tradition.

Many conservative sects in New England reacted strongly against holiday observances of the Church of England, and some of the holidays such as Christmas thus became a time of fasting rather than feasting. These days of abstinence may have reflected not only religious beliefs, but were rooted in the very early days when food was scarce and fasting was a matter of necessity and not one of choice.

As America moved into the eighteenth century and the population of the northeast increased, local customs began to reflect not only the somber beliefs of early residents, but the more liberal attitudes of settlers from other sections of Europe.

A dinner eaten by Massachusetts Judge Sewall included a multitude of dishes and was equal to the grandest feast given in the southern colonies, though it was by no means typical of New England life. The menu included boiled pork, boiled pigeons, boiled venison, roast beef, roast lamb, roast fowl, joil of salmon, oysters, fish and oil, cunners, leg of pork, hog's cheek and suet, minced pie, green peas, barley, corn in milk, gingerbread, sugared almonds, glazed almonds, honey, curds and cream, sage cheese, chocolate, orange shaddocks, quinces, strawberries, cherries, and raspberries.

In early colonial years, weddings went basically unobserved except for some celebration by members of the immediate family, but in later years marriages came to include some special food preparation for guests outside the wedding party.

Puritan funerals, however, were the highlight and may have been unrivaled by any other celebration in the area of food consumption. In these days of hardship, death at any age was common and rarely unexpected. New Englanders considered funerals to be primarily social occasions rather than periods of saddened abstinence, and they took advantage of such opportunities.

Recipes & Cookbooks

Cookbooks were not common in the colonial household. Like the slave cook and poorer frontier woman, many middle class and aristocratic housewives were illiterate, and thus not able to read printed recipes.

Money was also a factor limiting the spread of cookbooks. The average settler was probably unable to afford any but the most basic books, such as a bible or farming manual, and thus the housewife was left to her own initiative in preparing meals. Word-of-mouth exchanges of recipes may have been practiced in cities, but was impractical on the sparsely inhabited frontier.

In some cases, recipes that were special favorites were written down in personal notebooks called family receipt books. Many of these volumes were passed down from mother to daughter, thus preserving the best creations of the colonial era for future generations.

But for those who could read and purchase professionally written material, two principal sources of cookbooks existed.

First, England provided volumes dealing specifically with cooking or general books on farm husbandry, which also included assorted recipes. The most popular of these may have been *The Family Dictionary: or Household Companion*, by Dr. William Salmon; *The Compleat Housewife or Accomplished Gentlewoman's Companion*, by E. Smith, and *The Art of Cookery, Made Plain and Easy*, by Hannah Glasse.

One problem, however, was that these books, written by Britishers, took no notice of the American food situation. Many ingredients common in England were rare commodities in the colonies. The reverse was also true, for many

View from Bushongo Tavern on the Baltimore road. American, engraving from *Columbia Magazine*, 1788. *Photo courtesy Library of Congress.*

of the most abundant American foods were not included because of the scarcity of the items in Britain.

A second source of cookbooks in colonial America was provided by native printers such as William Parks, a Williamsburg publisher who in 1742 released a volume called *The Compleat Housewife*. This book is believed to have been the first cookbook actually published in America and was merely a reprint of the earlier English version by E. Smith. Parks did not add recipes for American dishes to the text, but did delete some foreign foods that were unusual or impractical in the life of the colonial cook.

A bibliography of colonial cookbooks compiled for the American Antiquarian Society shows that prior to 1776, a total of six different cookbooks was issued by American printers. Most were reprints of English cookbooks with little or no modification made to meet American requirements. One widely used text of the day was Susannah Carter's 1772 volume entitled *The Frugal Housewife*.

Several of the six books were printed in more than one edition, indicating that a market did exist for cookbooks in the colonies. Unfortunately, no

Village of the Sasquesahanok, German engraving from *Die Nieue Nonbekannte*, 1671.
Photo courtesy Library of Congress.

copies are known to exist now from the majority of these printings. Their one-time existence is known only through newspaper advertisements of the day, or references in the writings of this period.

Following the Revolution, Americans were no longer dependent upon British authors and publishers, so local writers began to codify dishes that had long been prepared in this country. The first cookbook published in America and written by an American author for American use did not appear until 1796. This book, written by Amelia Simmons who described herself as an American orphan, was entitled *American Cookery.*

Though brief, this first effort at recording American cuisine was important for it signaled the first time that recipes for foods such as pumpkin pudding, crooknecked squash, hoecakes, slapjacks, and Indian pudding had been included in a formal cookbook.

A great flood of native cookery volumes began appearing around the turn of the nineteenth century. It was in these volumes that many recipes for dishes that had been prepared for nearly one hundred and fifty years finally found their way into print. Most cookbooks printed after 1825, however, did not reflect the tastes and styles of the earlier colonial period.

After the first quarter of the new century, America's ties with France were reflected deeply in the country's food and eating habits, a fact that did not exist in prewar times.

Published recipes were not guaranteed to be either successful or tasty, for the science of measurement had yet to be applied to cooking. A quartern could mean either one-fourth of a peck, a bushel, a gill, a pound, or a pint. A teacup measure could vary by several ounces from household to household according to the drinking vessels of each family, and a spoonful could mean almost any small amount.

The lack of cookbooks, of standard measurements, difficulties in securing and preserving food, and the crude colonial cooking methods made meal preparation no simple task. Yet a thorough knowledge of food may have been unsurpassed in importance during these times of man's dependence upon nature for survival. The bounty of America's forests, streams, and meadows allowed the colonists to live.

Sugar, Spices, & Condiments

Christopher Columbus brought not only the *Niña*, *Pinta*, and *Santa Maria* to the New World, but sugar as well. A primary mission of his 1493 journey was to establish a sugar industry by transporting cane from his father-in-law's plantation in the Canary Islands to promising areas in the Caribbean.

Although Columbus's attempts did not succeed in establishing a profitable operation for his family's holdings, cane plants were soon flourishing throughout Central America and the West Indies. England began producing large quantities of refined sugar in Barbados about one hundred fifty years after Columbus's voyage, and much of the English crop production was sent to the American colonies for sale.

White processed sugar was expensive in America, so its use in most settlers' households was reserved for special occasions. Originally, sugar was packaged in solid, cone-shaped blocks weighing about ten pounds each. In the home, blocks were cut into smaller chunks by using special wrenchlike nippers, and then pounded into granular form for cooking.

An added bonus for the housekeeper was the dark blue paper in which sugar was wrapped for shipping, for the indigo colored tissues were highly valued as a home dye for clothing.

Molasses was a low-cost by-product of the sugar-refining process and, therefore, was used in the colonies more widely than the prime white sweetener. High sugar prices were the result not only of the immense profits claimed by island growers, but also stemmed from the complicated process of sugar-refining.

After the cane had been harvested and mashed, the raw juices were

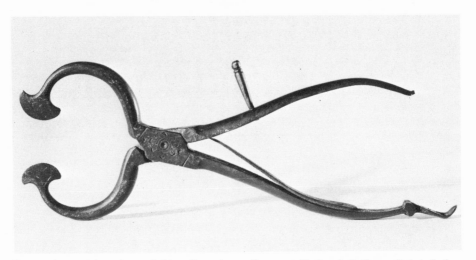

Sugar nippers. American, eighteenth century. *Courtesy National Gallery of Art, Index of American Design.*

boiled to extract sucrose or sugar. The syrup that remained after sugar had been crystallized was called first molasses. This brown syrup was then thinned with water and boiled again, so that more sugar could be removed. The residue from this second boiling was called second molasses.

Thus the sweetness, whiteness, and price of any grade of molasses was dependent upon the number of times that the raw cane juice had been boiled, adulterated with water, and the sugar removed. Blackstrap was the name usually given to the final syrup left after four or more boilings had been performed. Although blackstrap is lowest in sugar, it is highest in concentrated vitamins and minerals, a fact that helps to explain its current popularity as a health food.

An additional sweetener provided by the refining process was treacle, a liquid that drained from the refined sugar drying in molds. The syrup was also called sugarhouse molasses and was even lower in price than blackstrap.

Although molasses was widely used in colonial cooking, its greatest appeal was in French Creole regions after sugarcane became a major crop in Louisiana during the mid-eighteenth century. In other sections of the South, molasses was all important as a sweetener, for this syrup and salt were usually the only flavorings included in the food rations of slaves.

Honey could be gathered wild in the forests and used as a sweetener, but the supply was limited and long hours of searching were required to find a single comb. Some Indians claimed that bees were not known in America until the coming of European settlers who maintained extensive hives. As a result, the country's red men nicknamed the sometimes pesky insects English flies. Seventeenth-century naturalists, however, believed honey to be an ancient Indian food and included among the lists of indigenous American flora a specific plant called the Indian Hony Tree. This may have been a locust but whatever its identification the tree was sometimes pictured as a favorite target of an animal called the heyrat. This brown, catlike animal evidently spent much of his time raiding hives located in the honey tree.

Early colonists seeking to find an inexpensive and readily available source of sweetening adopted Indian methods and began tapping native sapbearing trees. Maple sugar and syrup were undoubtedly the earliest and most widely used sweeteners.

Sugaring-off time in Massachusetts and in other northern areas was a festive occasion when the whole settlement became involved in tapping trees, transporting the raw sap, and boiling the syrup and sugar. Approximately thirty-five gallons of sap were required for one gallon of syrup and the yield was even lower for maple sugar.

The Indian Hony Tree, by John Parkinson. English, woodcut, 1640. Courtesy The Garden Library, Dumbarton Oaks, Washington, D.C.

Salt, used for both preserving and disguising the taste of rotting meat, was perhaps the most important element in the colonial kitchen. For the wealthy, salt was imported from Portuguese islands in the Atlantic and from the West Indies. More modest households used bay salt, made from ocean water that had been allowed to evaporate naturally or in specially constructed reservoirs around which fires were built. As the frontier moved farther west away from the sea, settlers followed animal trails that led to natural salt licks near streams.

The ingenuity of housewives was severely tested when it came to flavoring, for the colonies were definitely not the herb and spice centers originally sought by explorers. Transportation costs for seasonings were high, and the settlers were so poor that basic flavorings in most pioneer houses came primarily from wild plants and trees.

Onions, celery, and cresses sprouted in marshy areas. Rosemary was always available either for cooking or for rubbing on the head in hopes that it would restore hair to bald areas. Garlic grew readily, while dandelions were picked not only as fresh salad greens, but dried and ground as a zesty touch in meat dishes. Horseradish was widely produced from the grated roots of a type of mustard plant, but was curiously avoided by most Indians. Settlers also found pot marjoram, thyme, milkweed, purslane, aniseed, chervil, chives, pennyroyal, winter sorrel, savory, liverwort, parsley, and leeks growing near their homes.

Sassafras, rhubarb, and several members of the mint family were plentiful, and were used not only in cooking, but in preparing beverages. One of the most popular was the wild bergamot mint, used by the Oswego Indians to brew

Iron pot used for boiling salt water into crystal salt. American, early eighteenth century. *Courtesy National Gallery of Art, Index of American Design.*

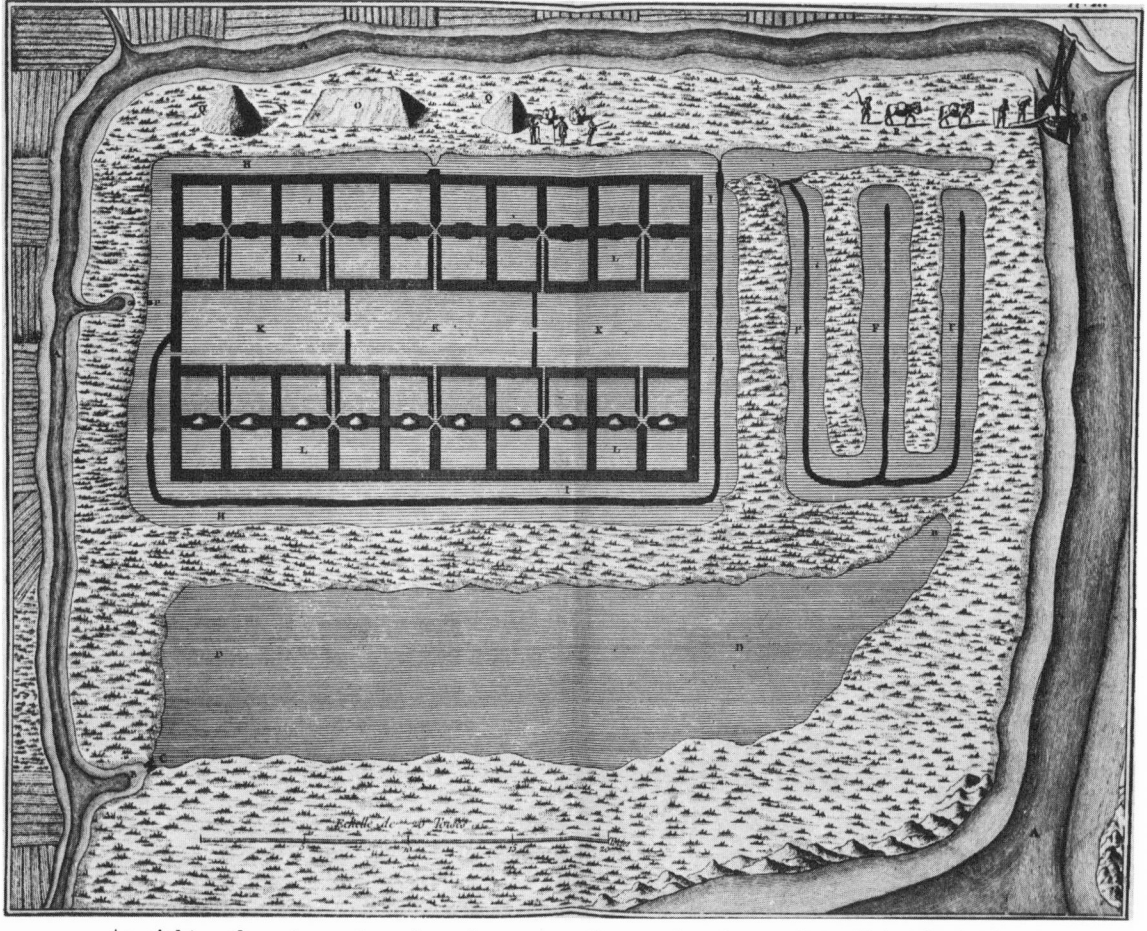

An eighteenth-century plan of a solar-evaporating works where salt could be obtained on a large scale. *Copied by The Mariners Museum, Newport News, Virginia.*

tea. During the American boycott of English products, the Oswegos shared their brewing techniques with revolutionary colonists who refused to purchase British teas.

Both the Indians and colonists relied upon the dried leaves, buds, and roots of flowers for aromatic seasonings. Marigolds, nasturtiums, geraniums, and several types of roses were carefully nourished in garden plots. Parts of the sunflower plant were ground as herbal products and the flower's oil was extracted for cooking. To Europeans this Indian staple was called the Golden Flower of Peru or the Flower of the Sun.

Horse Raddish; Dittander; Round Onions; Long Onions; Leekes; Garlicke; Rampions; Goates beard, by John Parkinson. English, woodcut, 1629. *Courtesy The Garden Library, Dumbarton Oaks, Washington, D.C.*

1 *Chryfanthemum Creticum.* Corne Marigolds of Candy. 2 *Flos Solis.* The Flower of the Sunne. 3 *Calendula.* Marigolds. 4 *After Atticus fine italorum.* The purple Marigold. 5 *Pilofella maior.* Golden Moufe-eare. 6 *Scorfonera Hifpanica.* Spanifh Vipers graffe. 7 *Tragopogon.* Goates beard, or goe to bed at noone.

Corn Marigolds of Candy; The Flower of the Sunne; Marigolds; The purple Marigold; Golden Mouse-eare; Spanish Vipess grasse; Goates beard, or goe to bed at noone, by John Parkinson. English, woodcut, 1629. *Courtesy The Garden Library, Dumbarton Oaks, Washington, D.C.*

The Small Water Lilly, by John Parkinson. English, woodcut, 1640. *Courtesy The Garden Library, Dumbarton Oaks, Washington, D.C.*

Indians also used yellow pond lilies for flavoring in dishes such as boiled liver. The fragile jack-in-the-pulpit was boiled and baked by Indian families so often that settlers called the flower Indian turnips. Early berries of the plant were used as flavoring with fresh venison.

The native American seasoning chart was completed with flavoring substitutes such as vinegar, wines, dried berries, ground nuts, and catsups of a wide variety.

Soon imported spices and herbs were available to those who could afford the high prices and whose ethnic cooking required an array of mixed flavors. Southern cooking, a highly seasoned blend of Latin, English, French, and African tastes, required large quantities of herbs. In the North, the pickled delicacies of German, Swiss, and Scotch settlers necessitated a wide variety of spicy accents.

England served as America's supplier of spice products from the Pacific spice islands, India, and herbal centers in the Mediterranean. Most colonials were charged elaborate prices for this service.

British merchants paid high insurance rates on ships crossing the Atlantic,

Wooden mortar and pestle used
for powdering whole spices. Seventeenth century. *Courtesy National Gallery of Art, Index of
American Design.*

and these costs were in turn passed along to the colonial consumer. For the
shipper who chanced a crossing without insurance, icebergs, hurricanes, rock
ledges, or pirates could mean the complete loss of cargo, crew, and ship. Such
financial calamities were compensated for by much higher profits on subse-
quent voyages. Losses could also spring from carelessly packaged ground
spices that were particularly susceptible to damage from seawater or rain.
Consequently, most spices were transported in their whole, natural state and
were ground after delivery, either by the local middleman who added a price
for his services or by the housewife who purchased the whole spice.

Hazards of the high seas also made it impossible for merchants to maintain
a complete line of imported products. As a result, spices were probably purchased in bulk form when they were available rather than when they were
needed.

Parsley; Smallage; Fenell; Dill; Chervill; Common Chervill, by John Parkinson. English, woodcut, 1629. *Courtesy The Garden Library, Dumbarton Oaks, Washington, D.C.*

5 *Sinapi,* Mustard. 6 *Asparagus,* Asparagus or Sperage.

1 *Portulaca,* Purſlane. 2 *Draco herba ſeu Tarchon,* Tarragon. 3 *Eruca ſativa,* Garden Rocket. 4 *Naſturtium ſativum,* Garden Creſſes.

1 *Maioranamaior Anglica.* Pot Marierome. 2 *Thymum vulgatius.* Garden Tyme. 3 *Satureia.* Sauorie. 4 *Hyssopus.* Hyssope. 5 *Pulegium.* Penniroyall. 6 *Salvia maior.* Common Sage. 7 *Salvia minor primata.* Sage of vertue.

Pot Marierome; Garden Tyme; Sauorie; Hyssope; Pennroyall; Common Sage;
Sage of vertue, by John Parkinson. English, woodcut, 1629. *Courtesy The Garden
Library, Dumbarton Oaks, Washington, D.C.*

Juft Imported from LONDON,

IN THE

Ship *ESTHER*, ROBERT SAVAGE, Commander,

And to be fold by

ALEXANDER HOME, at his Store in *BASSETERRE*,

VIZ.

Column 1

OATS and Beans
Brown, white and blue Oznabrigs
Pomerania Linnen
Princeß Linnen
Dowlas
Irish Linnens
Tandem Hollands
Cambricks
Clear Lawns
Diaper Table Cloths
Napkining Diaper
India Nankeens
Dimities
White Callico
Humhums
Chints
Ruffia Drabs
3-4ths wide Garlix
Tabling Huckaback
Cotton Romals
Blue Carradaries
Muquetta Netting
Bandannoes
India and China Silk Handkerchiefs
Strip'd Cotton Ginghams
China Taffety of different Colours
Women and Girls Stuff Coats
Luftrings
Padualoy
Short Mantua
Single and double Allopeens
Check Linnens
Check Cottons
Cotton Hollands
Linnen Handkerchiefs
White Jeans
Holland and dyed Jeans
Dinities
Cotton Counterpains
Quilts
Grandefize
Blue and green Cotton
Mahogany Bureaus
Ditto Dining Tables
Ditto Tea Tables
Ditto Tea Chefts
Book Ditto
Mahogany Voiders
Mens Knit Thread Hole
Womens knit and wove Ditto
Girls and Boys ditto
Black and white Silk Stockings
Worfted Breeches Pieces with Trimmings

Column 2

Silk Ditto
Silk Purfes
Worfted and Cotton Caps
Gold and Silver fcollop'd Laced Hats
Mens and Boys plain Hats
Superfine Hyfon, Green, and Bohea Teas
Single and double refin'd Sugar
Currants and Raifins
Cinnamon, Mace, Cloves and Nutmegs
Starch and Fig Blue
Patterns of fuperfine Broad Cloth of all Colours, with Trimmings
Mens Demy - Peak and Hunting Saddles
Huning Side Saddles
Curb and Snaffle Bridles
Woollen Surfingles
Curry and Main Combs
Brushes
Double and fingle Girths
Whips of all Kinds
Mens Shoes and Pumps
Morocco Slippers
Boys and Girls Shoes and Pumps
Womens Callimanco and Leather Shoes
Girls ditto
Gloves of all Sorts
Welton's high and low dry'd Snuff
Pigtail and cut Tobacco
Brown Thread
Superfine fitching ditto of all Kinds
Tapes and Ferrits
Plain and figur'd Ribbons of all kinds and Colours
Buttons of all Kinds
Laces of all Kinds
Needles and Pins
Womens newfl fashioned Ribbon'd
Hats, plain and figur'd
Tiffue ditto
Gold and Silver Lace
Me and Worns new-fashioned
Silver Buckle
Womens black Velvet laced Bonnets
W mens Satin Hats
Gauze Shades and Dophinettes
Stomachers of al Kinds
All Sorts of Chia Ware
Hard Metal Plats and Dishes
Stone, Glafs, all Earthen Ware of all kinds

Column 3

A Café of Silver Handle Knives and Forks in a Shagreen-cafe
Ivory Handle Knives and Forks in Mahogany Cafes
Horn and Ivory Handle Knives and Forks
Penknives
Steel Scifiars
Snuffers
Pencils
Needle-cafes and Thimbles
Powder-boxes and Combs
Cork-ferews
Buckles and Buttons of all Kinds
Snuff-boxes
Beads and Fans
Gilt and Silver Seals with Cornelians
Money Scales
Writing Paper
Ink-Powder
Dutch Quills
Playing Cards
Sealing Wax and Wafers
Merchants Books
Ink-ftands and Pounce-boxes
Tin Coffee-pots
Extinguifhers
Sauccpans
Lanthorns
Tinder-boxes
Kettles
Sugar-boxes
Boiling Houfe Lamps
Hair and Scented Powder
Lavender and Honey Waters
Walh-balls
Durham Muftard
Rappee Snuff
Corks
Turlington's Balfam of Life
Trunks of all Sizes
Hoes and Bills
Skimmers and Ladles
Iron Pots
ks of all Kinds   4d. 6d. 8d. 10d. 20d. and 30d. Nails
Kettles with Lamps
Coffee-pots
Copper Lamps
Brafs Cocks and Candlefticks
Hooks and Hinges
Coopers, Carpenters, Smiths, and Mafons Tools of all Kinds

In most areas, local herb gardens were planted in an attempt to bypass the uncertainties and high cost of direct purchasing of imported spices. America's soil was so well suited to herb growing that within a very few years after colonization plants that were traditionally used in European cooking were flourishing even in the colonial wilds. The lack of adequate records on indigenous plants, however, makes it difficult to determine exactly what herbs were native to the colonies and which were first imported.

Sage, licorice, chervil, caraway, dill, endive, red pepper, and basil may have been brought at first by immigrants, but rapidly took hold in local gardens.

Angelica, summer sorrel, fennel, horehound, and coriander also grew abundantly in this country's soil, but their origins have not been firmly established.

Journals and explorers' reports from America frequently mention flourishing plants, but modern-day identification of their colorful titles is difficult. No common nomenclature governed the naming of plants, and so a plant known by a particular name in one region probably had another name elsewhere. Self-heal, mouse-ear, eyebright, live-forever, Good-King-Henry, clown's allheal, lady's bedstraw, and feverfew are several frequently named plants. Whether these were eaten is not known.

The severe climate in the northern colonies prevented home growing of such choice tropical seasonings as ginger, samphire, pepper, cloves, mace, cinnamon, nutmeg, and allspice. Items such as capers, olive oil, lime juice, prunes, anchovies, and saffron were also available, but at prices so high as to all but prohibit their use in the average home.

Imported spices and seeds for herbs, vegetables, and fruits could be bought from local merchants or from apothecary shops in larger towns. On July 26, 1631, Plymouth's John Winthrop, Jr., purchased one pound, six shillings' worth of seeds from grocer Robert Hill. The bill shows that Winthrop selected more than fifty varieties of plant seeds, probably for use in his own garden.

As the colonies became more populated, urban grocers set up full-time shops, and in rural areas farmers sold produce at crossroad stands. In even the most elaborate establishments, food was sold alongside firewood, clothing, and other furnishings for the home. Among the merchants advertising their wares was a Mrs. Goose who peddled groceries in Salem, Massachusetts, and

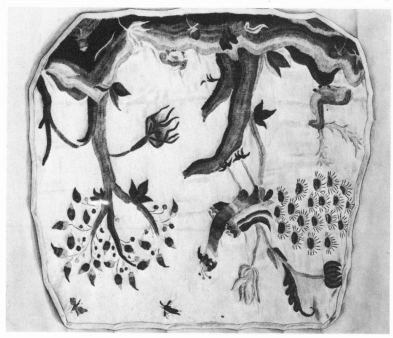

Crewelwork chair seat depicting deer, rooster and rabbit in the woods. Worked by Anne Bradstreet during the late seventeenth or early eighteenth centuries. Colored wool on cotton and linen. American. *Courtesy National Gallery of Art, Index of American Design.*

a Mistress Stagg in Williamsburg who specialized in hartshorn and calf's-foot jellies. Although not connected with the sale of food, the names of two other colonial women must be recognized along with Mrs. Goose and Mistress Stagg. They are Mrs. Mary Crabb, who lived near Fisher's wharf in Boston and did needlework, and Mary Salmon of the same city who shod horses.

A European view of American animals. Irish, 1737. From *The Natural History of North-Carolina. Photo courtesy Library of Congress.*

Meats

Deer, squirrel, and rabbit were probably the most common wild meat for early settlers, but diaries indicate that anything that ran and could be caught was regarded as a potentially edible item.

One Virginia explorer recorded that beaver was generally tough and dry, except for the tail; polecat was sweet; and the raccoon was not only higher in relish than mutton, but was also good for rubbing on swellings and inflammations of the body. Wildcat, unlike the otter which was eaten only in times of near famine, was favorably compared to veal, though sweeter and more delicate. Buffalo, which occasionally lumbered through northeast America and helped to clear footpaths in the dense forests, were sought-after targets for the hunter's bow or gun, until the burly animals moved west toward the open plains.

But most highly desired was wild bear meat, which was described as very savory and ''least apt to rise'' in the stomach. Both Indians and white men alike praised bear not only for its flavor, but because they believed great sexual prowess was given to those who ate its meat. This failing, bear was still worth the trouble of a hunt for its oil could be used as a mosquito repellent.

Wild meat pies and hashes helped to sustain thousands of new arrivals until vegetable crops could be planted and harvested; but before the colonists' first century in America had passed, towns began to legislate game laws regulating the hunting and trapping of larger animals. As early as 1646 Portsmouth, Rhode Island, closed deer-hunting season for six months of the year. Other areas soon followed suit.

These game laws helped in part to preserve the great numbers of game animals that were rapidly being diminished by commercial trappers hunting for pelts.

During the early eighteenth century, thousands of carcasses from wild animals were left untouched, while their more valuable skins were sent to Europe for clothing and other manufacturing items. For example, nearly one million deerskins were sent from South Carolina alone to England during the first fifteen years of the century. In 1748, the figure was 160,000 skins. A century before, America's woods teemed with white-tailed deer. One early Jamestown resident estimated that 200,000 such animals roamed on the tiny island and herds of up to 50 were not uncommon.

Increased attention to agriculture also helped to decrease the great wild herds of large game. As forests were cleared for planting, animals such as the elk and moose were gradually driven farther west in search of uninhabited areas where food was more abundant. As a result, the number of small game animals increased in the settled, cutover territories, and dishes featuring woodchuck, fox, hare, opossum, and raccoon became more popular.

Rattlesnakes also provided a ready meat source, but were eaten primarily by Indians who captured the sleeping reptiles with a forked stick. After the poisonous fangs were taken out, the snake's head was chopped off, the skin removed, and the remaining meat roasted over an open fire.

North American flora and fauna, including buffalo, stork, and opossum. Engraving from *Nouvelle Découverte,* 1697. *Photo courtesy Library of Congress.*

Leaping Deer. Artist unknown, American, steel pen drawing, c. 1840. *Courtesy Abby Aldrich Rockefeller Folk Art Collection, Williamsburg, Virginia.*

Domesticated livestock helped to fill the gap left by depletion of large wild animal herds. Upkeep for domestic stock was minimal since the animals were simply turned loose in the woods to graze and to be watched over peri-odically by a volunteer farmer from the nearest community. In the evening, herds were driven home to be milked or sheltered. When volunteers were lack-ing, some settlers constructed elaborate effigies of men near the grazing areas in an attempt to scare away marauding panthers and wolves. The sole expense in raising domestic meat was for salt, which was placed on the ground near the owner's house, not only because it was needed in the animal's diet, but to make sure that the stock remained in the farm's general area.

The price colonists paid for this low cost of raising stock was tougher meat because the animals became muscular and sinewy in the forest. Recipes

An eighteenth-century farm scene. American, woodcut from magazine, c. 1796. *Photo courtesy Library of Congress.*

commonly call for the housewife to vigorously pound her meat cuts with ax handles, hammers, and rolling pins in order to soften the sinewy roasts.

Sheep were domesticated in most areas by 1650, but were not eaten widely for nearly fifty years because of their more important value in supplying wool for clothing. One seventeenth-century cookbook attempted to satisfy the craving for lamb by a recipe for turning a pig into a lamb through an elaborate process of boiling and roasting: "This metamorphosis may at first seem somewhat strange," suggested Dr. Salmon, the book's author, "though we can assure you it has been much in esteem, viz. to make a Lamb out of a Pig . . ."

The rise of a cotton industry in the South and increases in the size of herds made both lamb and mutton available for general eating during the 1700s. By 1760, patriot John Adams recorded in his diary, amid deep thoughts on the theory of government, a description of a pleasant afternoon of fishing, highlighted by a picnic of mutton and "cyder." Despite the increase in availability, mutton and lamb never gained the popularity in the colonies that they had enjoyed in England where wild game was more difficult to acquire.

In most colonies cattle became domesticated in less than thirty years after the first family arrived. But these animals were rarely eaten for they were expensive to buy, useful as work animals, and necessary in breeding additional stock for sale. During the economic boom of the 1620s and early 1630s, large numbers of immigrating Puritans boosted the selling price of a single cow to nearly $1,400. Calves were sold in Massachusetts Colony for $500 and milk goats for $200. As the first wave of immigration subsided, prices tumbled to a more moderate $250 for a cow and $45 for a goat.

Later, money was perhaps not as important as rare foodstuffs, for settlers arriving in Maryland were urged to bring wine, sugar, prunes, raisins, currants, honey, and spices to trade for cattle and other domestic animals. Even after herds became more numerous, beef was primarily a meat for wealthy or middle-class colonists and was only rarely eaten by the poorer colonists. Large roasts of beef were either boiled, roasted, or baked, but many

The Unwelcome Customer, by J. Collet, English, 1772. Courtesy Colonial Williamsburg, Williamsburg, Virginia.

settlers preferred the animal's head, tongue, bone marrow, and sweetbreads to the tougher cuts. A special delicacy was the pluck that included the animal's heart, liver, and lungs. A hashlike dish called bubble and squeak was produced from strips of beef fried with cabbage.

Pigs, often used to pull carts, were undoubtedly the most widely eaten domestic meat and the hog was a valuable asset in any house. Like cattle, pigs traditionally ran wild in the woods, eating roots and nuts, or milled about in village streets consuming garbage. The situation became so unsanitary in New York communities that residents adopted the Dutch door, which could be latched at the bottom to keep the pigs from the house, but could be open at the top to let in fresh air.

When later settlers penned their hogs, much of the distinctive flavor may have been removed from the pork meat. One eighteenth-century connoisseur stoutly maintained that the delicious taste of Virginia hams stemmed from the large number of snakes consumed by pigs feeding in the woods. Hogpens, however, did help to eliminate a sore point of contention between settlers and local Indians, whose unfenced gardens were often destroyed by free-roaming pigs. Whites also complained of pig vandalism, and so in 1636 a hogreeve was appointed in Boston. Like today's dogcatcher, his job was to round up strays. Nearly thirty years later, the General Assembly authorized construction of a hog pound in neighboring Newport.

William Byrd of Westover, Virginia, during his colonial travels, commented frequently upon the North Carolina custom of consuming huge amounts of pork, and speculated that local residents were developing hoglike tendencies. One entry in his journals declares:

The truth of it is, these people live so much upon the swine's flesh that it don't only incline them to the yaws and consequently to the downfall of their noses, but makes them likewise extremely hoggish in their temper, and many of them seem to grunt rather than speak in their ordinary conversation.

Everything but the pig's squeal was useful for eating or making household items. The choice rib and loin sections were roasted, while the jowls and fat were salted for cooking with vegetables. A pig's knuckles and head were pickled, innards made into spicy hog's pudding, and feet jellied into aspic.

Small prime scraps of pork were chopped fine, lightly seasoned, and fried into a sausage for dessert. A hog's bristles were used as brushes, his tallow for candles, and his hide for clothing. Even the blood of a newly butchered pig was saved to produce black pudding. In this dish, a container of fresh blood was stirred until cold to prevent clotting, then thickened with meal and spiced with herbs. The final product was smoked and cured like bacon.

Slaughtering time was of great importance to early settlers and was a day of community celebration as well as work. Pigs chosen to be butchered, usually by shooting, were identified by special rings inserted in their noses or by ear-marks branded when they were shoats.

Because of the great value placed on each part of the pig and the difficul-ties involved in preserving freshly slaughtered meat, settlers would often give large amounts of the kill to their neighbors. The family receiving such a bonanza was naturally expected to return the favor when it slaughtered its own stock.

There were practical restrictions on the methods of preparing not only pork, but any large cut of meat. Hashes, ragouts, and soups, which were called potages, were particularly favored dishes in these early days when knives were a rarity and the most common eating utensil was a wooden spoon or a shell.

Even some prime sections of beef had to be pounded, mashed, or chopped so that dishes could be eaten easily. The first minced meat pies were indeed made from minced or ground meats of several types, and many recipes re-

Trade sign of the butcher Reed. American, painted wood, c. 1850. Courtesy The Shelburne Mu-seum, Inc., Shelburne, Vermont.

Indians hunting rabbits and foxes. Flemish engraving from Theodor de Bry's *America,* 1624. *Photo courtesy Library of Congress.*

quired balls or round mashed meat patties highly seasoned with spices. When large cuts of fresh meat were considered tender enough to be cooked whole, the roast, when done, would be thoroughly diced into bite-sized cubes before being brought to the table.

Such difficulties did not confront the Atlantic coast Indians who never maintained extensive herds of domestic animals and survived primarily on day to day hunting forays. Some tribes did raise dogs for eating, but man's best friend was probably consumed only on special occasions such as religious festivals.

Both legend and sacred taboos influenced the cooking techniques of almost every tribe, particularly those groups that depended heavily upon hunting.

One widespread belief was that if a dinner pot contained both the beasts of the ground and the birds of the air, then the forest gods would be provoked into driving away all game. Thus, most red men rejected the mixed pots or hotchpots, which were the favorite dishes of white settlers.

Many tribes worshiped gods who periodically appeared in animal form such as snakes or rabbits. These meats were, of course, taboo. Young braves on their first hunt dared not consume the first animal they slew, for it was understood that the penalty for such an act would be permanent bad luck at hunting.

Perhaps the most frequently held belief was the existence of the animal soul that could communicate with other wildlife both before and after death. As a result, detailed rituals were observed in the hunting, killing, and eating of wild game. The idea was that if an animal's carcass was treated without respect, its soul would warn the other living game to flee the Indian hunters. Elaborate ceremonies where braves praised the beauty, valor, and goodness of the kill were aimed at prompting the animal's soul to pass a message to other beasts that they would be treated fairly if killed.

A ''first fish'' ceremony was also practiced in some areas. Here, the idea was that the first fish caught would be so impressed with the reverence shown by the Indians, that it would urge the rest of his school to swim into the nets. Some tribes developed a system that assured food for members of the community who were not great hunters or fishermen. On a mass tribal foray, the brave who actually brought down the kill was allowed the prime parts, but the first hunter to actually touch the animal received the next best share. In this way a poor marksman, if he was swift of foot, could still provide for his family. In addition, visitors to an Indian dwelling were traditionally offered food during their stay, thus making the abode of the tribe's best hunter a popular place during times of famine.

Mass hunting matches were held during the severe winter months. Unlike the fair weather season when game abounded in the forests near permanent villages, Indians in cold climates were forced to travel great distances to obtain food. Bows and arrows and spears were the most common hunting implements until guns were obtained from settlers. Often packs of Indian dogs, a crossbreed between domesticated species and wolves, were used to tree small animals or attack bear and elk.

A special technique was reserved for the moose. Hunters would closely watch quiet ponds where the animals frequently gathered to feed on the roots of floating lilies. When the moose's head was well beneath the water, the kill would be made, thus eliminating the need for a tiring chase through the forest.

The manner of their attire and painting themselves when they goe to their generall huntings or at theire Solemne feasts.

An Indian brave whose body has been decorated with symbolic painting appropriate for a hunting match or a festival, by John White. English, watercolor, c. 1577–1590. *Photo courtesy Library of Congress.*

Game and fish were all important in the diet of most tribes. Generations of living close to nature had revealed that many obscure items such as wasp nymphs could sustain man in times of famine. Deer was probably the mainstay of the Indian diet, and even unborn fawns were removed from slaughtered does and cooked in their own bags. During long winters when the supply of smoked or salted meat ran low, some tribes brewed a soup from dried buckskin, smoke, and snow.

Some Europeans scorned many native dishes such as "tyger," which was eaten only by "savages." Wolves also received their share of disparaging remarks, but settlers did admit that wolf meat was a helpful cure for gout. Bats were considered abominable to settlers, but were sometimes fed to the children of the poor, to blacks, and to "savages."

The disdain for unorthodox food was not shared by all newcomers, particularly those who had been near starvation, such as Elizabeth Hard. Mrs. Hard, an early settler of Pennsylvania, described her great pleasure when her pet cat dragged home a large dead rabbit. She promptly prepared English hare, a welcomed treat after days of surviving on biscuits and cheese.

Not all colonial hunters were free to pursue the great numbers of wild game. Because of the widespread fear of slave insurrection, southern colonists passed special codes severely limiting the right of Negro and Indian servants to carry guns.

In most areas, the slaves were allowed to hunt if accompanied by their master. Special tickets or passes were granted which enabled the slave to track beyond the boundaries of his own plantation home. But even in northern colonies such as New Jersey, there were strict statutes that limited the times and places during which a slave could hunt with dogs and guns. In the same state, a 1760 law prohibited slaves from setting traps above a certain size. In New England where rebellion was less likely, the reverse was often found. Blacks were constantly armed and sent into the woods to bag the master's dinner. Rather than a crime, hunting was here almost compulsory.

The raising of domestic animals by slaves was also restricted. City ordinances in South Kingstown, Rhode Island, provided a penalty of thirty-one lashes to any Negro owning pigs, cows, or other stock. Boston magistrates as late as 1746 could levy a fine of twenty shillings on any person renting a pigsty to an Indian, Negro, or mulatto without the consent of the owner. In the South, laws tended to be colony wide rather than local. The 1712 slave code of South Carolina prohibited any slave from keeping hogs, cattle, or horses. Penalties may have been quite severe, since instead of specifying the exact punishment, these laws left sentencing to a local board of white citizens.

In the South, slaves were allowed to raise small animals, such as chickens, because of economic conditions. Near the end of the colonial period and until the Civil War, many owners of large plantations allowed and perhaps compelled slaves to produce as much of their own foodstuffs as was possible. The rationale was to relieve the owner of his obligation to provide slave food rations, and also to make a slave more hesitant to run away because of his vested interest in owning animals.

As a result of legal restrictions, meat eating among slaves never became widespread or common. After the Revolution, one segment of American writers maintained that the treatment of slaves was much improved over the harsh conditions imposed during the colonial period. At this same time, however, a French observer noted that meat was provided to blacks less than six times a year, and that most lived primarily on Indian corn and infrequent allotments of buttermilk. While the exact estimate may vary, meat at a slave meal was always the exception rather than the rule. At no time did its consumption approach the high volume eaten by white Americans who depended so heavily upon high protein dishes for their survival.

Indians hunting deer while disguised under buckskins, 1564. Engraving after Frenchman Jacques Le Moyne de Morgues, 1591. *Photo courtesy Library of Congress.*

Meat Recipes

BEEF

TO RAGOUT A PIECE OF BEEF CALLED BEEF A-LA-MODE Take a buttock of beef, interlaced with good lard, rolled up with chopped spice, sage, parsley, thyme, and green onions; put it into a great sauce pan, and bind it close with coarse tape. When it is half done, turn it, let it stand over the fire on a stove twelve hours. It is fit to be eat cold or hot.

When it is cold, slice it out thin, and toss it up in a fine ragout of sweet-breads, oysters, mushrooms, and palates.

The Frugal Housewife, 1772

TO BOIL BEEF OR MUTTON When your meat is put in, and the pot boils, take care to scum it very clean, otherwise the scum will boil down, stick to your meat, and make it look black. Send up your dish with turnips, greens, potatoes or carrots. If it be a leg or loin of mutton, you may also put melted butter and capers in a boat.

The Frugal Housewife, 1772

TO MAKE GLUE BROTH Take a leg of beef, veal, venison or any other young meat, because old meat will not so easily jelly. Pare off all the fat, in which there is no nutriment, and of the lean make a very strong broth after the usual manner, by boiling the meat to rags till all the goodness be out.

After skimming off what fat remains, pour the broth into a wide stewpan, well tinned, and let it simmer over a gentle, even fire till it comes to a thick jelly. Then take it off and set it over boiling water, which is an evener heat and not so apt to burn the broth to the vessel. Over that let it evaporate, stirring it very often till it be reduced, when cold, into a solid substance like glue. Then cut it into small pieces, laying them single in the cold, that they may dry the sooner.

When the pieces are perfectly dry, put them into a canister, and they will be good, if kept dry, a whole East India voyage.

The Prose Works of William Byrd of Westover

TO MAKE MINCED MEAT PIE   Shred a pound of neats tongue parboiled, with two pounds of beef suet, five pippins, and a green lemon peel. Season it with an ounce of spice, a little salt, a pound of sugar, two pounds of currents, half a pint of sack, a little orange-flower water, the juice of three or four lemons, a quarter of a pound of citron, lemon and orange peel. Mix these together and fill the pies.

The Frugal Housewife, 1772

TO ROAST BEEF   The general rules are, to have a brisk hot fire, to hang down rather than to spit, to baste with salt and water, and one quarter of an hour to every pound of beef, tho' tender beef will require less, while old tough beef will require more roasting, pricking with a fork will determine you whether done or not; rare done is the healthiest and the taste of this age.

American Cookery, 1796

TO ROAST SWEETBREADS   Parboil two large ones; when cold, lard them with bacon, and roast them in a Dutch oven. For sauce, plain butter and mushroom catsup.

The American Domestic Cookery, 1822

TO MAKE SWEETBREAD RAGOUT   Cut them about the size of a walnut, wash and dry them, then fry them of a fine brown; pour to them a good gravy, season with salt, pepper, allspice, and either mushrooms or mushroom catsup; strain, and thicken with butter and a little flour.

The American Domestic Cookery, 1822

TO BOIL A NEAT'S TONGUE   A dried tongue should be soaked over night, when you dress it, put it into cold water and let it have room; it will take at least four hours. A green tongue out of the pickle need not be soaked, but will require near the same time. An hour before you dish it up, take it out and blanch it, then put it into the pot again till you want it, this will make it eat the tenderer.

The Frugal Housewife, 1772

TO DRY TONGUES Take to every two ounces of salt-petre, a pint of petre-salt, and rub it well, after it is finely beaten, over your tongue, and then beat a pint of bay-salt, and rub that on over it, and every three days turn it; and when it has lain nine or ten days, hang it in wood smoke to dry. Do a hog's head this way.

For a ham of pork or mutton, have a quart of bay-salt, half a pound of petre-salt, a quarter of a pound of salt-petre, a quarter of a pound of brown sugar, all beaten very fine, mix'd together, and rubbed well over it. Let it lie a fortnight; turn it often, and then hang it up a day to drain, and dry it in wood smoke.

The Compleat Housewife, 1730

HARE

TO MAKE HARE PIE Cut the hare in pieces, break the bones, and lay them in the pie. Lay on balls, sliced lemon, and butter, and close it with the yolks of hard eggs.

The Frugal Housewife, 1772

TO JUG A HARE Having cased the hare, turn the blood out of the body into the jug. Then cut the hare to pieces, but do not wash it. Then cut three quarters of a pound of fat bacon into three slices.

Pour upon the blood about a pint of strong, old, pale beer: put into the jug a middling sized onion stuck with three or four cloves, and a bunch of sweet herbs. And having seasoned the hare with pepper, salt and nutmeg, and lemon peel grated, put in the meat, a layer of hare, and a layer of bacon. Then stop the jug close, so that the steam be kept in entirely.

Put the jug into a kettle of water over the fire, and let it stew three hours, then strain off the liquor, and having thickened it with burnt butter, serve it up hot, garnished with lemon sliced.

New American Cookery, 1805

TO STEW A HARE Beat it well with a rolling pin in its own blood. Cut it into little bits and fry them. Then put the hare into a stew pan with a quart of strong gravy, pepper and salt according to the palate, and let it stew till tender. Thicken it with butter and flour. Serve it up in its gravy with sippets in the dish and lemon sliced for garnish.

The Frugal Housewife, 1772

LAMB AND MUTTON

TO FIX LAMB Leg boiled in a cloth to look as white as possible: the loin fried in steaks and served round, garnished with dried or fried parsley. Spinach to eat with it. Or dressed separately or roasted.

A New System of Domestic Cookery, 1807

TO FRY LAMB Separate the leg from the loin, cut off the shank and boil the leg; divide the loin in chops, dredge and fry them a nice brown, lay the leg in the middle of the dish and put the chops around, pour over parsley and butter and garnish with fried parsley.

The leg cut into steaks and the loin into chops will make a fine fricassee or cutlets.

The Virginia Housewife, 1825

AN EXCELLENT HOTCH POTCH Stew pease, lettuce, and onions, in a very little water, with a beef or ham bone. While doing, fry some mutton or lamb steaks, seasoned, of a nice brown. Three quarters of an hour before dinner put the steaks into a stew pan, and the vegetables over: stew them, and serve them all together in a tureen.

Another Hotch Potch—Knuckle of veal, and scrag of mutton, stewed with vegetables as above.

A New System of Domestic Cookery, 1807

TO BOIL BREAST OF MUTTON Separate the joints of the brisket, and saw off the sharp ends of the ribs, dredge it with flour, and boil it. Serve it up covered with onions.

The Virginia Housewife, 1825

TO ROAST MUTTON If a breast let it be cauled, if a leg, stuffed or not, let it be done more gently than beef, and done more; the chine, saddle or leg, re-quire more fire and longer time than the breast. Garnish with scraped horse radish, and serve with potatoes, beans, colliflowers, water-cresses or boiled onions, caper sauce, mashed turnips, or lettuce.

The New England Cookery, 1808

TO MAKE FORCED MEAT Take part of a leg of mutton, veal or beef, and pick off the skins and fat, and to every pound of meat put in two pounds of beef-suet. Shred them together very fine, then season it with pepper, salt, cloves, mace, nutmeg, and sage. Then put all into a stone mortar, and to every two pounds of meat put half a pint of oysters and six eggs well beaten. Then mix them all together and beat it very well. Then keep it in an earthen pot for your use. Put a little flour on the top, and when you roll them up flour your hands.

The Compleat Housewife, 1730

PORK

TO MAKE BEST BACON To each ham put one ounce salt-petre, one pint bay salt, one pint molasses, shake together six or eight weeks, or when a large quantity is together, baste them with the liquor every day. When taken out to dry, smoke three weeks with cobs or malt fumes.

American Cookery, 1796

TO COLLAR A PIG   Slit the pig down the back, take out all the bones, wash the blood in three or four waters, wipe it dry and season it with savory spice, thyme, parsley and salt and roll it in a hard collar. Tye it close in a dry cloth, and boil it with the bones in three pints of water, a handful of salt, a quart of vinegar, a faggot of sweet herbs, whole spice, a penny-worth of ising-glass. When it is boil'd tender, take it off, and when cold, take it out of the cloth, and keep it in this pickle.

The Compleat Housewife, 1730

TO SOUSE PIG'S FEET AND EARS   After you have cleaned your pigs feet and ears, boil them till they are tender; then boil as much spring water, with salt and vinegar in it, as will cover them. When both are cold, put the feet and ears into a pan, and pour the pickle over them; and when you use them, take them out, split them in two, and lay them in a dish. Chop some green parsley and shalott fine, mix it with oil and vinegar, and a spoonful of mustard, and pour over them; or put them into a batter and fry them. Serve with butter and mustard in a boat.

The New England Cookery, 1808

TO CURE HAMS   Hang them a day or two; then sprinkle with a little salt, and drain them another day. Pound an ounce and a half of salt petre, ditto petre salt, half an ounce sal prunel, and a pound of the coarsest sugar. Mix these well, and rub into each ham every day for four days, and turn it. If a small one, turn it every day for three weeks: if a large one, a week longer; but do not rub after four days. Before you dry it, drain and cover with bran. Smoke it ten days.

A New System of Domestic Cookery, 1807

TO MAKE PORKER'S HEAD ROASTED   Choose a fine young head, clean it well, and put bread and sage as for pig. Sew it up tight, and put it on a string or hanging jack. Roast it as a pig, and serve with the same sauce.

A New System of Domestic Cookery, 1807

TO RAGOUT HOG'S FEET AND EARS If they are raw or fowled, boil the feet and ears till they are tender, after which cut them into thin bits about two inches long and a quarter of an inch thick. Put them into a stew pan with half a pint of good gravy, a glass of red wine, a good piece of butter rolled in flour, a little pepper and salt, a good deal of mustard, and half an onion. Stir all together till it becomes of a fine thickness and then pour it into a dish, meat and gravy together.

The Frugal Housewife, 1772

TO BOIL A LEG OF PORK A leg of pork must lie in salt six or seven days after which put it into a pot to be boiled, without using any means to freshen it. It requires much water to swim in over the fire, and also to be fully boiled; so that care should be taken that the fire do not slacken while it is dressing. Serve it with melted butter, mustard, buttered turnips, carrots or greens.
N.B. The other joints of the swine are most commonly roasted.

The New England Cookery, 1808

TO STUFF A LEG OF PORK Corn the leg forty-eight hours and stuff it with sausage meat and bake in an oven two hours and a half or roast.

The New England Cookery, 1808

TO COOK SAUSAGES Take half a pound of sausages and six apples. Slice four about as thick as a crown, cut the other two in quarters. Fry them with the sausages of a fine light brown, and lay the sausages in the middle of the dish, and the apples round. Garnish with the quartered apples.

The New England Cookery, 1808

TO MAKE SAUSAGES Chop fat and lean of pork. Season with sage, pepper and salt; and you may add two or three pimentos. Half fill hog's guts that have been soaked and made extremely clean: or the meat may be kept in a very small pan, closely covered; and so rolled and dusted with a very little flour before they are fried.

A New System of Domestic Cookery, 1807

TO ROAST A FOREQUARTER OF SHOTE Joint it for the convenience of carving, roast it before a brisk fire. When done, take the skin off, dredge and froth it, put a little melted butter with some caper vinegar over it, or serve it with mint sauce.

The Virginia Housewife, 1825

TO MAKE A LAMB FROM A PIG This metamorphosis may at first seem somewhat strange, though we can assure you it has been much in esteem, viz. to make a Lamb out of a Pig, in this manner:

Take a fat pig, scald him, and cut off the head, slit him, and truss him up like a lamb. Then being slit through the middle, and flea'd, boil him a while: then being draw'd with parsley, as you do for lamb, roast it, and it will not be easily discern'd from lamb.

The Family Dictionary, 1705

VEAL

TO DRESS A CALF'S HEAD Scald the hair off, and take out the bones; then have in readiness palates boiled tender, the yolks of hard eggs, oysters scalded, and forc'd meat; stuff all this into your head, and sew it up close in a cloth. Boil it three hours; make a strong gravy for sauce, and garnish with fried bacon.

The Compleat Housewife, 1730

TO BOIL CHINE Cut the chine in three or four pieces, and lard them with small lard. Season them with salt, and broil them, laying under them some sprigs of rosemary, bay-leaves, and sage. Dust them over with a little flour; and being broiled, serve them up with gravy, the juice of limon, and beaten butter.

The Family Dictionary, 1705

TO MAKE KNUCKLE OF VEAL   Boil a half pint of pearl barley in salt and water till quite tender. Drain the water from it and stir in a piece of butter, put it in a deep dish, have the knuckle nicely boiled in milk and water, and lay it on the barley, pour some parsley and butter over it.

The Virginia Housewife, 1825

TO MAKE LITTLE PASTIES TO FRY   Take the kidney of a loin of veal or lamb, fat and all; shred it very small; season it with a little salt, cloves, mace, nutmeg, all beaten small, some sugar, and the yolks of two or three hard eggs, minced very fine. Mix all these together with a little sack or cream; put them in a puff-paste and fry them; serve them hot.

The Compleat Housewife, 1730

TO MAKE VEAL GRAVY   To make white gravy, take part of a knuckle of veal, or the worst part of a neck of veal, boil about a pound of this in a quart of water, an onion, some whole pepper, six cloves, a little salt, a bunch of sweet herbs, half a nutmeg sliced; let them boil an hour and then strain it off and keep for use.

The Frugal Housewife, 1772

TO MAKE LUMBER PIE   Take a pound and a half fillet of veal, mince it with the same quantity of beef suet, season it with sweet spice, five pippins, a handful of spinach and a hard lettuce, thyme and parsley. Mix it with a penny loaf grated and the yolks of two or three eggs, sack and orange-flower water, sweet spice, a pound and a half currents and preserves, and a caudle.

The Frugal Housewife, 1772

VENISON

TO BOIL A HAUNCH OF VENISON   Salt the haunch well, and let it lay a week. Then boil it with a cauliflower, some turnips, young cabbages, and beet roots: lay your venison in the dish, dispose the garden things round it in separate plates, and send it to the table.

The New England Cookery, 1808

HASHED VENISON Should be warmed with its own gravy, or some without seasoning as before; and only warmed through, not boiled. If there is not fat left, cut some slices of mutton fat, set it on the fire with a little port wine and sugar, simmer till dry; then put to the hash, and it will eat as well as the fat of the venison.

The American Domestic Cookery, 1822

TO ROAST VENISON A haunch of buck will take about three hours and three quarters roasting; doe three hours and a quarter. Put a coarse paste of brown flour and water, and a paper over that, to cover all the fat. Baste it well with drippings and keep it at a distance to get hot at the bone by degrees. When nearly done, remove the covering, and baste it with butter, and froth it up before you serve.

A New System of Domestic Cookery, 1807

TO MAKE VENISON PASTY Raise a high round pie, shred a pound of beef suet, and put it into the bottom; cut your venison in pieces and season it with pepper and salt. Lay it on the suet, lay on butter, close the pie, and bake it.

The New England Cookery, 1808

TO RECOVER VENISON WHEN IT STINKS Take as much cold water in a tub as will cover it a handful over, and put in good store of salt, and let it lie three or four hours. Then take your venison out, and let it lie in as much hot water and salt, and let it lie as long as before. Then have your crust in readiness, and take it out and dry it very well, and season it with pepper and salt pretty high, and put it in your pastry. Do not use the bones of your venison for gravy, but get fresh beef or other bones.

The Compleat Housewife, 1730

Fowl

Chickens are believed to have been introduced into the colonies at Jamestown about 1607, and by 1700 were so plentiful that they were no longer recorded on inventories of family property.

Most chickens were simply roasted, but a more festive dish was chicken fricasseed in rich brown gravy with wild herbs. The forerunner of modern fried poultry was a concoction named pulled chicken, which involved jerking large chunks of raw meat from the bird's bones and browning the morsels in deep fat.

With a frugalness that characterized all early housewives, the innards were saved from chickens that had been either roasted, fricasseed, or pulled as the essential ingredients for the next day's meal. These tough livers, gizzards, and hearts were chopped fine, highly seasoned, and then baked in a paste made from flour, water, and lard. The result was the early American version of chicken pot pie.

Eggs from chickens and other fowl such as wild plovers were eaten by all economic classes, but were usually not served at breakfast time. Most colonists preferred their eggs either poached, stewed, battered, or fried, and then served as a side dish at dinner or supper. Hard-boiled eggs, when sliced and mixed with bone marrow, provided filling for a dinner pasty. Also popular as a main dish was boiled eggs salmagundi. For this rather elaborate item, yolks were removed from the eggs and the whites served with an assortment of chopped leftover meats, vegetables, and nuts. If laid on Christmas Day, eggs prepared in any manner were a special treat, particularly for those Dutch groups who believed such eggs when eaten would reduce a hernia.

Peacocks, imported into Jamestown at the same time as chickens, were

A European view of American fowl. Irish, 1737. From *The Natural History of North Carolina. Photo courtesy Library of Congress.*

bred less successfully for food, and a later attempt to introduce pheasants and partridges into the colonies also failed. The experiment, conducted on a New Jersey estate owned by Benjamin Franklin's son-in-law, Richard Bache, was halted when the entire pheasant flock failed to survive the first year's winter. Within several years after the country's settlement, however, geese and ducks became domesticated and large backyard flocks provided settlers with poultry on a year-round basis.

Falcons, hawks, eagles, and buzzards, though never domesticated, were hunted widely as food sources, as was almost any type of songbird. Some of these, which were evidently well known in colonial days, are difficult to recog-nize today because of the informal names often applied to early American wildlife. One bird, identified as a wobble, was described as an ill-shaped fowl that had no long feathers, looked like a penguin, and was unable to fly. The bird was fat in the spring and was extremely oily when roasted or stewed. If this was not sufficient to strain the credibility of colonial naturalists, another widely recognized bird called a loone had similar characteristics.

Near the sea and on inland rivers, wild waterfowl were plentiful every-where during most seasons, with teals, cranes, herons, swans, geese, and ducks frequently roasted or stewed into soup. Numerous variations for cooking these birds grew up in the area around Chesapeake Bay, where waterfowl wintered, eating the wild celery plants that flourished in the marshy bogs.

Wild birds were prepared much like chicken, but with a shorter cooking time. Recipes ranged from a simple roasted bird to an elaborate potted fowl, which was preserved in containers of highly flavored gelatin. In addition to providing settlers with an abundant supply of foodstuffs, wildfowl were also indispensable as a source of household necessities such as down for mattresses and quills for writing pens.

Colonial terminology for the carving of fowl was considerably more com-plicated than today. In prerevolutionary times, specific names were given to the slicing of each type of bird. A swan was "lifted"; a goose "broken"; hens were "spoiled"; a mallard "unbraced"; pigeons were "winged"; and wood-cocks "thighed."

Turkeys were plentiful throughout the year and their importance as a food can scarcely be overemphasized. Many patriotic citizens during the selec-tion of a national bird to symbolize America's characteristics originally favored the great wild turkey, which was more common to colonials than the rarer bald eagle.

Ardea Caeruiea (Blue Heron), by Mark Catesby. English, hand-colored engraving, c. 1731–1743. *Courtesy Colonial Williamsburg, Williamsburg, Virginia.*

Benjamin Franklin, supported by James Madison, led the turkey lobbyists and soundly condemned both the bad moral character and the predatory hunting habits of the eagle. Supporters of the gobbler's rival, however, carried the day in the Continental Congress when in the heat of debate it was alleged that the turkey was both cowardly and stupid, and therefore not typical of the bold new nation. The discussion, not one of the most critical problems faced by the Congress during the Revolution, raged for six years.

Size estimates of wild turkeys ranged up to fifty pounds, but like the deer, this bird's abundance quickly diminished. One reason was extensive hunting by colonists. Another factor in the decline was the practice of early settlers to gather the wild ginseng berry, a favorite turkey food. Unlike most other berries, ginseng was not eaten locally, but the plant and roots were exported profitably to the Chinese drug market where it was processed into a medicinal narcotic.

Traveler John Josselyn recognized the potential demise of the turkey as early as 1672. In his book *New-Englands Rarities*, a slim volume listing the weirdities of colonial life, Josselyn wrote:

. . . I have also seen threescore broods of young Turkies on the side of a marsh, sunning of themselves in a morning betimes, but this was thirty years since, the English and the Indian having now destroyed the breed, so that 'tis very rare to meet with a wild Turkie in the woods . . .

Successful efforts were made to maintain the distinctive flavor of the wild turkey. Early housewives hunted eggs in the forests and the young chicks were later bred to domestic strains, thus producing a cross match of flavors.

Shooting, English, hand-colored engraving, 1779. Courtesy Colonial Williamsburg, Williamsburg, Virginia.

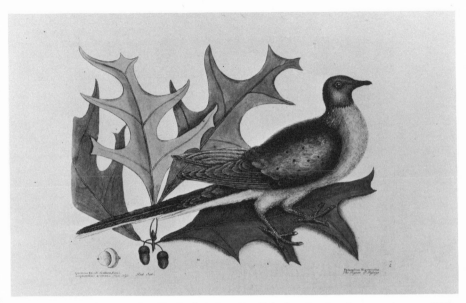

The Pigeon of Passage, by Mark Catesby. English, hand-colored engraving, c. 1731–1743. *Courtesy Colonial Williamsburg, Williamsburg, Virginia.*

Ironically the passenger pigeon, probably the most widely eaten bird in colonial times, is now extinct. For many centuries, North American Indians valued this most numerous of all fowls, not only for its sweet flesh, but for its oil, which was used in cooking. One Indian village of seventeen families is recorded as having in storage at least one hundred gallons of the bird oil.

Colonial reports of the birds' great numbers border on the unbelievable. One such report was penned by North Carolina historian John Lawson, who described the flight of 1701–1702. In this massive invasion by pigeons, Lawson wrote that limbs were torn from trees by the weight of millions of roosting birds. Large areas of land were completely ravaged for food. A later description of a similar flight, which also included Virginia, was made by artist-naturalist Mark Catesby. He claimed that great oaks were toppled by the birds, which were so numerous as to roost on top of one another. The droppings supposedly covered the ground to a depth of four inches and every acorn for miles was eaten, thus complicating the food problem for free-roaming hogs searching for their meals.

The Summer Duck, by Mark Catesby. English, hand-colored engraving, c. 1731–1743. Courtesy Colonial Williamsburg, Williamsburg, Virginia.

Journals of the Plymouth settlers suggest that this colony also suffered from the birds' hunger. Reports state that the settlers feared a severe winter famine in 1643 because great hordes of pigeons had consumed most of the year's grain crop. Audubon recorded periods in the nineteenth century when flock were so dense as to block out the sun like an eclipse, and he estimated that during one three hour counting period he observed more than one billion, one hundred million pigeons pass overhead as part of a three day flight. In the eighteenth century, colonists in Philadelphia and New York stood on their rooftops and balconies to shoot into great flocks as a sporting event.

The destruction of crops by the passenger pigeon was easily surpassed by man's slaughter of their great numbers. Settlers devised more efficient ways of bagging many birds at a single hunting session. One of the most popular involved using blinded pigeons staked to the ground as decoys to lure whole flocks from the sky. Then nets would be dropped and as many as fifteen hundred birds could be caught at once. In order to save gunpowder and balls, the birds were clubbed to death.

Early cookbooks are filled with scores of recipes for preparing passenger pigeons in every conceivable manner. The birds were stewed, fricasseed, fried, boiled, roasted, hashed, cooked into pies, and preserved. But for the present-day cook, these formulas are simply reminders of an animal who has passed from the scene. Martha, the last of the passenger pigeons, died on September 1, 1914, at the Cincinnati Zoological Park.

Another fowl that failed to survive the settler's hunting techniques was the heath hen. This grouse-type bird was also numerous during the colonial era, but decreased rapidly in numbers during the nineteenth century. Its final refuge was a retreat on Martha's Vineyard where it was nurtured under strict protection.

Indications are that the bird was widely eaten in prerevolutionary times. Servants in Boston are recorded as protesting that their meals were too dependent upon the heath hen and demanded more variety. But like the passenger pigeon, attempts to save the few remaining hens were unsuccessful and it too was erased from the records of living species.

Quail, grouse, woodcock, plover, curlew, and even larks were eaten by American pioneers, but unlike the passenger pigeon and the heath hen, their numbers increased. As more and more dense forests were cleared and fields planted in grain, flocks of these birds rapidly multiplied and their descendants are with us today.

Many of the birds hunted for colonial cooking pots are now protected by federal migratory laws and vigorously enforced state statutes. Thus, today's cooks may never have the opportunity of sampling roasted robin or bobolink stew. But recipes for fowl such as chicken and turkey, together with legally hunted game birds, can be re-created as deliciously today as they were hundreds of years ago.

Fowl Recipes

DOMESTIC FOWL

TO FORCE COCK'S COMBS Parboil your cock's combs, then open them
with a point of a knife at the grate-end. Take the white of a fowl, as much
bacon and beef-marrow, cut these small and beat them fine in a marble mortar.
Season them with salt, pepper and grated nutmeg, and mix it up with an egg.
Fill the combs and stew them in a little strong gravy softly for half an hour.
Then slice in some fresh mushrooms, and a few pickled ones; then beat up the
yolk of an egg in a little gravy stirring it, season it with salt. When they are
enough, dish them up in little dishes or plates.

The Art of Cookery, 1747

TO FRICASSEE CHICKEN Cut up the chickens raw, in the manner as you
do for eating, and flat the pieces a little with a rolling pin. Fry them of a light
brown; afterwards put them into a stew pan, with sufficient quantity but not
too much gravy, a spoonful or two of white wine, to two or three chickens,
a little nutmeg and salt. Thicken it with flour and butter. Garnish with sippets within the dish, and with crisp parsley on the rim.

The Frugal Housewife, 1772

TO PULL CHICKEN Take off the skin and pull the flesh off the bones of
a cold fowl, in as large pieces as you can. Dredge with flour, and fry of a nice
brown in butter; which drain from it, and simmer in a good gravy, well seasoned and thickened with a little flour and butter. Add the juice of half a
lemon.

A New System of Domestic Cookery, 1807

TO ROAST YOUNG CHICKENS   When you kill young chickens, pluck them very carefully, truss and put them down to a good fire. Dredge and baste them with lard, they will take a quarter of an hour in roasting; froth them up, lay them on a dish, pour butter and parsley on them, and serve them up hot.

The Virginia Housewife, 1825

AN EGG PIE   Shred the yolks of twenty hard eggs with the same quantity of marrow and beef suet; season it with sweet spice, citron, orange and lemon; fill and close the pie.

The New England Cookery, 1808

TO POACH EGGS   Set a stew pan of water on the fire; when boiling, slip an egg, previously broken into a cup, into the water, when the white looks done enough, slide an egg slice under the egg, and lay it on toast and butter or spinach.

A New System of Domestic Cookery, 1807

TO PRESERVE EGGS   May be preserved by anointing them with lard or any greasy or oily substance for months, and some say years. The oily substance closes the pores, hinders the access of air, and thus prevents putrefaction. They should be anointed soon after they are laid.

The Husbandman and Housewife, 1820

TO MAKE SMALL DISHES FOR SUPPER   Boil eggs hard, cut them in half. Take out the yolks, set the whites on a dish, and fill with the following several ingredients; or put them in a saucer upside down on a plate and place them in quarters round: in either case as a salmagundi. Chopped veal, yolk of egg, beet root, anchovy, apple, onion, ham and parsley. A very small bit of the white of the egg must be cut off, to make it stand on the dish as a cup.

A New System of Domestic Cookery, 1807

TO ROAST TURKEY, GOOSE, DUCK, FOWL, ETC. When you roast a turkey, goose, fowl or chicken, lay them down to a good fire. Singe them clean with white paper, baste them with butter, and dust on some flour.

As to time, a large turkey will take an hour and twenty minutes; a middling one a full hour, a full grown goose if young an hour; a large fowl three quarters of an hour; a middling one half an hour, and a small chicken twenty minutes; but this depends entirely on the goodness of your fire.

When your fowl are thoroughly plump and the smoke draws from the breast to the fire, you may be sure that they are very near done. Then baste them with butter; dust on a very little flour, and as soon as they have a good froth, serve them up.

Sauce for a turkey—Good gravy in a dish; and either bread, onion, or oyster sauce in a bason.

Sauce for a goose—A little good gravy in one bason and some apple-sauce in another.

For a duck—A little gravy in the dish and onions in a teacup.

Sauce for fowls—Parsley and butter; or gravy in the dish and either bread sauce, oyster sauce or egg sauce in a bason.

The Frugal Housewife, 1772

TO MAKE A TURKEY PIE Bone the turkey, season it with savory spice, and lay it in the pie, with two capons cut in pieces, to fill up the corners. A goose pie is made the same way, with two rabbits to fill it up as aforesaid.

The Frugal Housewife, 1772

TO STUFF A TURKEY Grate a wheat loaf, one quarter of a pound butter, one quarter of a pound salt pork, finely chopped, two eggs, a little sweet marjoram, summer savory, parsley, pepper and salt (If the pork be not sufficiently) fill the bird and sew it up. The same will answer for all wild fowl. Water fowls require onions. The same ingredients stuff a leg of veal, fresh pork, or a loin of veal.

New American Cookery, 1805

WILD LAND BIRDS

TO ROAST GROUSE   Are to be roasted like fowls; but their heads twisted under the wing, and served with gravy, and bread sauce, or with sauce for wild fowl.

A New System of Domestic Cookery, 1807

TO ROAST LARKS   Truss your larks with the legs a-cross, and put a sage leaf over the breast; put them on a long fine skewer, and between every lark a little piece of thin bacon. Then tie the skewer to a spit, and roast them at a quick clear fire. Baste them with butter and strew over them some crumbs of bread mixed with flour; fry some bread crumbs of a nice brown, in a bit of butter. Lay your larks round in your dish, the bread crumbs in the middle, with a sliced orange for garnish. Send good gravy in a dish.

The Frugal Housewife, 1772

TO COOK PHEASANTS AND PARTRIDGES   Roast as turkey, and serve with a fine gravy: in which put the smallest bit of garlick, and bread sauce. When cold, they may be made into excellent patties, but their flavor should not be over powered by lemon.

A New System of Domestic Cookery, 1807

TO STEW PIGEONS   Stuff the birds with seasoning made of ground pepper, salt, mace and sweet herbs. Half roast them, then put them in a stew pan with a sufficient quantity of gravy, a little white wine, some pickled mushrooms and lemon peel. When stewed enough, take out the birds, thicken the liquor with butter and the yolks of eggs.

The New England Cookery, 1808

TO BROIL PIGEONS   Slit them down the back: season and broil. Serve with mushroom sauce; or melted butter, with a little mushroom catsup.

A New System of Domestic Cookery, 1807

TO COOK WOODCOCKS, SNIPES AND QUAILS Roast them without drawing, and serve on toast. Butter only should be eaten with them as gravy takes off the fine flavor. The thigh and back are esteemed the most.

The American Domestic Cookery, 1823

WOODCOCK TO ROAST Being drawn, wash and truss them. Lay them to the fire, and baste them with butter; being all most enough, strew grated bread on them, and save the gravy into which you must put toast that are butter'd, or you may only mince the guts, being roasted with the fowl into the gravy and a little claret, and so serve them up.

The Family Dictionary, 1705

WATERFOWL

DUCK TO BOIL Choose a fine fat duck, salt it two days, then boil it slowly, and cover it with onion sauce made very white, and the butter melted with milk instead of water.

A New System of Domestic Cookery, 1807

GOOSE TO DRY Take a fair fat goose, powder it about a month, then hang it up in a chimney as you do bacon; and when it is thoroughly dry, boil it well and serve it to the table, with some mustard and sugar; garnish your dish with bay-leaves. Hogs cheeks are very good dried thus.

The Family Dictionary, 1705

TO STUFF AND ROAST A GOSLIN Boil the innards tender, chop them fine, put double quantity of grated bread, four ounces butter, salt (and sweet herbs if you like) two eggs moulded into the stuffing. Parboil four onions and chop them into the stuffing, add wine and roast the bird.

The New England Cookery, 1808

TO DRESS PLOVERS Roast the green ones in the same way as woodcocks and quail, without drawing; and serve on a toast. Gray plovers may be either roasted, or stewed with gravy, herbs and spice.

The American Domestic Cookery, 1822

TO FIX PLOVER'S EGGS Are a nice and fashionable dish. Boil them ten minutes and serve either hot or cold on a napkin.

The American Domestic Cookery, 1822

TO POT A SWAN Bone and skin your swan, and beat the flesh into a mortar, taking out the strings as you beat it. Then take some clear fat bacon and beat with the swan, and when 'tis of a light flesh colour, there is bacon enough in it; and when 'tis beaten till 'tis like dough, 'tis enough. Then season it with pepper, salt, cloves, mace and nutmeg, all beaten fine; mix it together with your flesh, and give it a beat or two all together.

Then put it in an earthen pot, with a little claret and fair water, and at the top two pounds of fresh butter spread over it. Cover it with coarse paste, and bake it with bread: then turn it out into a dish and squeeze it gently to get out the moisture; then put it in a pot fit for it and when cold, cover it over with clarified butter. The next day paper it up. In this manner you may do goose, duck, or beef or hare's flesh.

The Compleat Housewife, 1730

TO ROAST WIDGEON, DUCK, TEAL OR MOORHEN The flavor is best preserved without stuffing; but put some pepper, salt and a bit of butter in the birds. Wild fowl require to be much less done than tame, and to be served of a fine color.

The basting ordered takes off the fishy taste which wild fowl sometimes have. Send up a very good gravy in the dish; and on cutting the breast, half a lemon squeezed over, with pepper on it improves the taste.

Or stuff them with crumbs, a little shred onion, sage, pepper and salt, but not a large quantity, and add a bit of butter. Slice an onion, and put into the dripping pan, with a little salt, and baste the fowls with it till three parts done: then remove that, and baste with butter. They should come up finely frothed, and not be overdone.

A New System of Domestic Cookery, 1807

TO STEW WILD FOWL   Half roast a wild duck, etc. Then cut it into bits. When cold, put it into a stew pan, with a sufficient quantity of beef gravy, and let it stew till tender. Then thicken it with burnt butter, and serve it up altogether with sippets within the sides, and lemon sliced on the rim of the dish.

The Frugal Housewife, 1772

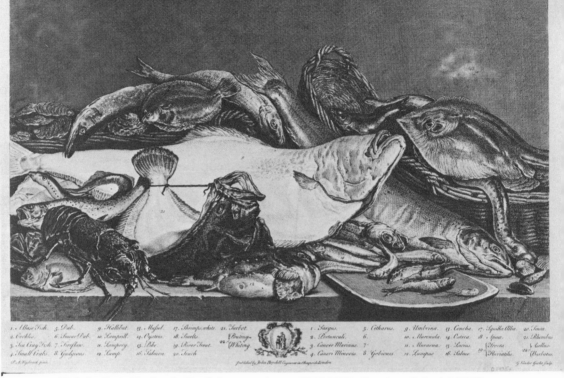

Fish, by P. A. Rysbrach. English, engraving, c. 1765–1775. *Courtesy Colonial Williamsburg, Williamsburg, Virginia.*

Seafood

From the earliest days of exploration, colonial settlements along the coast and inland waters depended heavily upon fish and crustaceans for subsistence.

One of the first meals eaten in America by passengers of the *Mayflower* included soft-shell clams, quahogs, and mussels, which caused the hardy band to "cast and sour."

Friends of early Plymouth leader Miles Standish soon discovered that the New England Indian diet also included various foods from the sea. One of the first recorded documents in American history details colonists' observations on the fare of an Indian village on Cape Cod. In addition to deer, one observer noted that the food in the native huts consisted of "two or three Baskets full of parched Acornes, peeces of fish and a peece of broyled Hering." At Pokanoket, capital of the Wampanoag nation, braves netted tautog fish and collected scallops, clams, and eels, which were cooked into a fish stew called nasaump.

But fish were not only to be found in northern bays. Years later Virginia historian Robert Beverley reported that he had eaten at least twenty-eight varieties of fish from Virginia waters alone.

Most middle-class English immigrants, whose old country mores often condemned fish-eating as a horrifying habit, quickly changed their customs. Scores of recipes were devised for preparing hundreds of American seafood items, but the results were not always pleasant. Reports indicate that several early pioneers died from eating sturgeon, probably due to ptomaine poisoning caused by insufficient storage methods. Colonial Virginia waters teemed with sturgeon, evidently anxious to be caught, for traveler David De Vries recorded that while boating to Jamestown, an eight-foot sturgeon leaped into his sloop.

New England codfish cakes and chowders were as popular three hundred years ago as they are today. Large fish, such as sturgeon, salmon, and the sharklike skate, were usually simmered several hours in large iron kettles filled with water and vinegar. Small species, such as bass, catfish, mullet, perch, flounder, pike, haddock, oldwives, and mackerel, were roasted, fried, or smoked for winter use. Fresh sounds, or the air sacs and swimming bladders of fish, were considered delicacies, particularly when boiled in milk and served with a rich cream sauce.

Shad ran in most waters along the mid-Atlantic coast and was cooked on a wooden board to absorb wood flavors. This planked shad is still a specialty of seafood restaurants around Chesapeake Bay. In many areas of the South, shad was not so highly prized and residents in some communities caught both buck and roe shad for hog feed.

Settlers soon adopted Indian methods for cooking eels and lampreys, which were so numerous that early writers claimed that huge basketfuls were caught with ease. For cooking, the long fish were first split lengthwise, then wrapped around a stout stick which was stuck upright in an open fire. Baby eels were coiled in tiny rings and fried in deep fat.

The sea also provided porpoise and manatee for the tables of colonists, and alligators were eaten in the southern colonies. Although the flesh was thought to be musky, the meat was a supposed cure for both ulcers and cancer.

Indians valued highly the grampus or black whale, which they called the howling whale. For at least two centuries before large-scale whaling fleets were launched from New England ports, nature's largest mammal was hunted in the Americas.

In 1625, European Samuel Purchas explained the routine method of whale fishing by "savages" of Florida. According to contemporary reports, Florida's Indians canoed into the ocean and, finding a suitable whale, swam alongside until a propitious moment when the animal sounded. Then the Indian leaped on the whale's back and riding astride began to pound a large stick into the blowhole. Additional sticks as needed were driven on top of the first, thus cutting off oxygen and causing fatal damage to the whale's inner organs. A line attached to the fins then allowed the Indians to drag their catch to shore where the meat was cut away, pounded, and dried for later use.

Sea turtles and terrapin were standard items in port towns such as Annapolis and New York, where citizens held special turtle and Madeira sup-

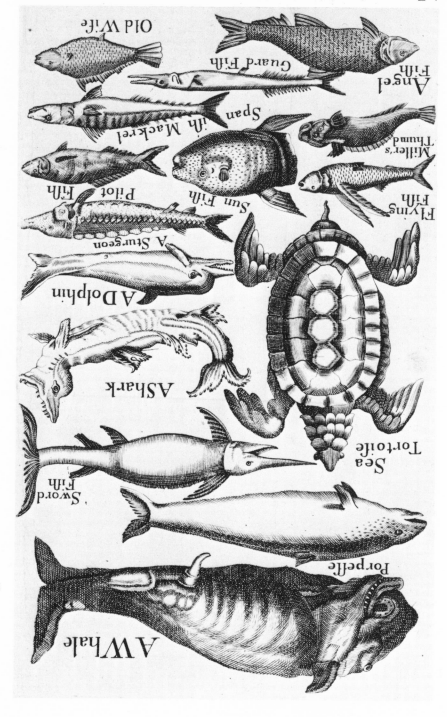

A European view of American fish. Irish, 1737. From *The Natural History of North Carolina*. Photo courtesy Library of Congress.

The Art of Dressing Fish.
German, mezzotint, 1772.
Courtesy Colonial Williamsburg, Williamsburg, Virginia.

pers. On Long Island, weekly turtle barbecues were attended by entire communities. To the south in Maryland, diamond-back terrapin were so numerous that slave owners were cautioned against feeding the animal to their workers more than three times a week.

Special calapash turtle in the shell was a favorite in South Carolina where turtle pens were often kept in backyards of houses. Turtle eggs, though tough and difficult to break, were said to be both sweet and invigorating to the constitution, and thus were widely served by colonial women to their husbands in the belief that it would give the men sexual virility.

Frogs, clams, periwinkles, conchs, oysters, scallops, cockles, and mussels made regular appearances at the table, and were either cooked alone or mixed with rice, potatoes, or bread. Maryland crab cakes and New England oyster stew are still prepared with the same ingredients used in oceanside villages centuries ago.

The Atlantic loggerhead turtle, by John White. English, watercolor, c. 1577-1590. Courtesy Trustees of The British Museum.

Usually, shellfish were simply roasted or stewed in their own juices, but some early recipes resulted in more elaborate creations. One colonial sauce included lobsters and crabs baked with parsley, pepper, walnuts, mace, butter, and lemon juice. Baked shellfish, such as clams, were sometimes served in long-handled bed warmers (if chafing dishes were not available), which were so popular in this period. Fresh shellfish were available to many settlers even during the most severe winters, for oysters and clams were kept alive for months inside of cabins when placed in special beds of wet sand and cornmeal.

Seafood was of prime importance to Indians who invented elaborate nets, hooks, lines, and floating traps for fishing. Tribes from the interior areas of New Jersey often walked for days to gather shellfish from the coast. After drying them in the sun, the catch was pickled and later used as a spiced flavoring in stews. Roger Williams, founder of Rhode Island, recorded that the Narragansett Indians valued a special type of clam broth, for it could be substituted for salt in flavoring corn breads and porridges.

Lobsters, today considered a delicacy in New England, were not held in such high esteem in colonial days. Indian women of the area dove for the spiny creatures, which were then used as bait for more desirable fish. To the south, natives were more anxious to eat lobsters and used roasted venison in their crawfish traps.

Fishing techniques were as varied as the nationalities of young America's settlers. Pole fishing was at first extremely unrefined. Early hooks were probably pieces of shell or bone with a barb whittled onto one end. Metal hooks were originally homemade items consisting of a piece of iron or tin bent and spiked with a hole in the top for the line. By the late seventeenth century, needle manufacturers in England began producing more sophisticated products, some of which were probably imported into the colonies.

Immigrants were urged to bring their own hooks, and the more foresighted were able to use their supply for rigging gang wires or floating lines on which several hooks were set at once.

Line on the frontier was produced from any type of string, animal gut, or hair. Rounded rocks served as sinkers, and even artificial lures were tried. Artificial bait was probably first used as a method for quickly catching a dinner without wasting the time to collect live bait.

Nets and traps were other primitive means of fishing by immigrants who also used frog gigs and harpoon irons. Wealthy colonials often bought made-

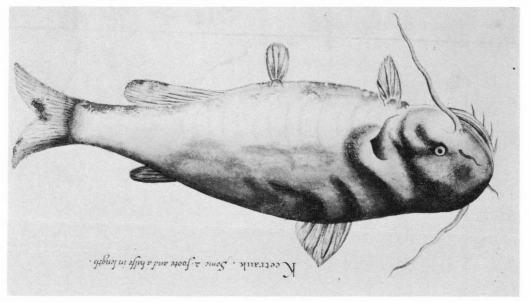

A catfish. Sloane copy of a John White watercolor. English, c. 1610. *Courtesy Trustees of The British Museum.*

to-order nets in England with special lead and cork parts used in trawling from boats.

Indians had long fashioned rather elaborate fishing apparatus, such as intricate nets made from woven grasses or animal sinews. Spears, gigs, and bows and arrows were common equipment, particularly for night fishing. One of the most prevalent techniques was with a weir, a loosely woven dam of reeds that was placed at a narrow point of a stream to trap fish but allowed the water to flow through.

When Benjamin Franklin warned in *Poor Richard's Almanac* that both fish and visitors smelled in three days, he was touching on a major problem confronting early settlers: food preservation. Keeping freshly killed or harvested food from spoiling for use in the winter was a puzzle that faced all inhabitants of the New World. It was of lifesaving importance in these times. Temporary preservation of fresh food was accomplished in several ways. In the South, special box houses were built over cool springs, while in the

Indians fishing by using several native devices, such as spears, traps, nets, and a weir, by John White. English, watercolor, c. 1577–1590. *Photo courtesy Library of Congress.*

North, settlers were able to freeze their goods in the snow. Buckets of food were suspended into wells, and special aboveground rooms called Dutch cellars were dug out of hillsides or earth mounds. Special coolers or brick-lined pits constructed in the basement of larger houses served as refrigerators. On plantations, special ice holes insulated with straw and sod were built. Ice cut from rivers and ponds frozen over during the winter could often last until autumn when stored in the temperate pits of the mid-Atlantic colonies. In the South, where ice was often shipped in from northern areas, the melting time was much shorter.

When meats left untended too long became tainted and developed unpleasant odors, spices were used with a heavy hand and were an essential part of cooking. But more satisfactory methods were needed to keep food unspoiled over long periods of time.

Smoking was one solution. Out of this slow curing of food over low fires made from hickory chips or corncobs came many famed creations. Special smokehouses in the South produced bacon that was often fried with rum, as well as sausages and whole hams called gammon. Gammon, as originally cooked, was soaked in fresh water for several days and then simmered in a slow pot for many hours. This process removed much of the salt and hickory taste of the smoked ham.

In New England and in Dutch New York, smoking was standard processing not only for pork, but for seafoods such as salmon, herring, and mackerel. Beef was also cured, and one New York farmer boasted that the beef roasts smoked by his wife were so compact that they were not sliced, but shaved with a carpenter's plane.

Pickling was a second and more expensive method of food preservation, for it required spices and herbs that had to be imported from the West Indies or from India via England. However, almost every staple in the early American diet was subject to this painstaking process. Fish, such as herrings, were kept unspoiled in vats of brine, and oysters were pickled in such great numbers that they were shipped to Barbados, thus becoming one of the first profitable exports of the New World.

Souse, headcheese, corned beef, and sauerkraut sustained thousands through winter famines. The most common pickling brines for meats and other products were made from either seawater or fresh water and salt from animal licks. Preserving in these heavy salt solutions was also known as brining or corning.

Salting, sometimes called powdering, and drying foods was a well-known preservation technique, particularly in rural or frontier towns where the spices required for pickling were often unobtainable. This process produced dried jerky and hardtack, items long associated with the later western movement, but actually eaten on the Atlantic coast during colonial times. Settlers may have learned the process from Indians, for the word jerky is derived from the Indian term charqui meaning dried meat.

In Massachusetts and Maine, salted sturgeon and onions were produced in large numbers for overseas consumption. Dried, salted cod from the same area and from Nova Scotia was the main source of protein for thousands of slaves in the West Indies sugar islands. A 1625 census at Jamestown indicated that salting was widespread in that area and in nearby settlements. For 1,232 persons counted by the census, there were 58,380 pounds of salted fish in storage.

The colonial cook would indeed be awed by modern conveniences in food preparation, but few improvements have been made upon her delectable recipes for serving the harvest of the sea.

Women salting and packing cod. Engraving from *Traité Générale des Pêches*, c. 1769–1777. *Photo courtesy Library of Congress.*

Seafood Recipes

TO MAKE CHOUDER Take a bass weighing four pounds, boil half an hour; take six slices raw salt pork, fry them till the lard is nearly extracted; one dozen crackers soaked in cold water five minutes. Put the bass into the lard, also the pieces of pork and crackers, cover close, and fry for twenty minutes; serve with potatoes, pickles, apple sauce or mangoes. Garnish with green parsley.

New American Cookery, 1805

TO DRESS COLD CRAB Empty the shells, and mix the flesh with oil, vinegar, salt, and a little white pepper and cayenne. Then put the mixture into the large shell and serve. Very little oil is necessary.

The American Domestic Cookery, 1822

TO MAKE HOT CRAB Pick the meat out of a crab, clear the shell from the head, then put in the former, with a very small bit of nutmeg, salt, pepper, a bit of butter, crumbs of bread, and three spoonfuls of vinegar, into the shell again, and set it before the fire. You may brown it with a salamander. Dry toast should be served to eat it upon.

A New System of Domestic Cookery, 1807

FOR DRESSING CODFISH Put the fish first into cold water, and wash it, then hang it over the fire and soak it six hours in scalding water, then shift it into clean warm water, and let it scald for one hour. It will be much better than to boil.

New American Cookery, 1805

TO BOIL COD SOUNDS Soak them in warm water half an hour, then scrape and clean, and if to be dressed white, boil them in milk and water. When tender, serve them in a napkin, with egg sauce. The salt must not be much soaked out, unless for fricassee.

The American Domestic Cookery, 1822

TO BOIL EELS The small ones are best. Do them in a small quantity of water, with a good deal of parsley, which should be served with them and the liquor. Served chopped parsley and butter for sauce.

TO MAKE EEL BROTH Very nourishing for the sick. Do as above; but stew two hours, and add an onion and peppercorns; salt to taste.

FRIED EELS If small, they should be curled round and fried, being first dipped into egg and crumbs of bread.

The American Domestic Cookery, 1822

TO MAKE EEL PIE Cut, wash and season them with sweet seasoning and a handful of currants, butter, and close it.

The Frugal Housewife, 1772

TO BROIL HERRINGS Floured first, and done of a good colour. Plain butter for sauce. They are very good potted like mackerel.

A New System of Domestic Cookery, 1807

TO SMOKE HERRINGS Clean, and lay them in salt and a little salt petre one night. Then hang them on a stick, through the eyes, in a row. Have ready an old cask, in which put some saw-dust, and in the midst of it a heater red-hot. Fix the stick over the smoke, and let them remain twenty-four hours.

The American Domestic Cookery, 1822

TO BAKE LAMPREYS Draw and split your lampreys, take out the strings in the back, flea them, and truss them around: then having parboiled them, let them be seasoned with pepper, nutmeg and salt. Place a laying of butter at the bottom of the pye, lay on the lampreys with some sliced onions, and covering it with butter, close it up; and when it is baked, fill up the pie with clarified butter.

The Family Dictionary, 1705

TO BUTTER LOBSTER Pick the meat out; cut it and warm with a little weak brown gravy, nutmeg, salt, pepper and butter, with a little flour. If done white, a little white gravy and cream.

A New System of Domestic Cookery, 1807

TO MAKE LOBSTER SALAD Make a salad; and put some of the red part of the lobster to it, cut. This forms a pretty contrast to the white and green of the vegetables. Do not put much oil, as shell-fish absorb the sharpness of vinegar. Serve in a dish, not a bowl.

The American Domestic Cookery, 1823

TO STEW LOBSTER Pick the lobster, put the berries into a dish that has a lamp, and rub them down with a bit of butter, two spoonfuls of any sort of gravy, one of soy or walnut catsup, a little salt and cayenne, and a spoonful of port. Stew the lobster cut in bits with the gravy. It must be dressed at the table and eaten immediately.

A New System of Domestic Cookery, 1807

TO FRY MUSCLES Put them into a kettle, in which there is as much boiling water as will cover them. Being enough, take them up and beard them, then wash them in warm water, wipe them dry and flour them. Being fried crisp, dish them up with butter beaten with the juice of lemon and parsley throwed over them, fried crisp and green.

The Family Dictionary, 1705

TO MAKE OYSTER PIE Parboil a quart of large oysters in their own liquor, mince them small, and pound them in a mortar, with pistachio nuts, marrow and sweet herbs, and onion and savory seeds, and a little grated bread; or season as aforesaid whole. Lay on butter and close it.

The Frugal Housewife, 1772

TO PICKLE OYSTERS   Take a quart of oysters, and wash them in their own liquor very well, till all the grittiness is out. Put them in a sauce pan or stew pan and strain the liquor over them. Set them on the fire, and scum them; then put in three or four blades of mace, a spoonful of whole pepper-corns, when you think they are boiled enough, throw in a glass of white wine.

Let them have a thorough scald; then take them up, and when they are cold, put them in a pot and pour the liquor over them, and keep them for use. Take them out with a spoon.

The Compleat Housewife, 1730

TO BOIL PERCH   Put them into cold water, boil them carefully and serve with melted butter and soy. Perch are a most delicate fish. They may be either fried or stewed, but in stewing they do not preserve so good a flavor.

The American Domestic Cookery, 1822

TO ROAST SALMON   Take a jole of salmon, or a rand, and divide it into four pieces. Season it with salt and grated nutmeg. Stick in it whole cloves and put it on a convenient spit, laying on it likewise a few bay leaves and sprigs of rosemary. Then baste it with butter and save the drippings to mingle with other butter, to be served in sauce, mixed with verjuice, the juice of oranges, and garnished with slices of orange.

The Family Dictionary, 1705

TO BROIL SHAD   Take a fresh shad, salt and pepper it well, broil half an hour; make a smoke with small chips while broiling. When done add butter, and wine if agreeable.

Salmon or any other kind of fresh fish may be prepared in the same manner.

New American Cookery, 1805

TO GRILL SHRIMPS Season them with salt and pepper. Shred parsley, butter and scallops-shells well; add one grated bread and let them stew for half an hour. Brown them with a hot iron and serve them up.

The Art of Cookery, 1747

TO MAKE SHRIMP SAUCE Wash half a pint of shrimps very clean. Mince and put them in a stew pan, with a spoonful of anchovy liquor and a pound of thick melted butter; boil it up for five minutes and squeeze in half a lemon. Toss it up and put it in a sauce boat.

The Virginia Housewife, 1825

TO SPIT SPRATS When cleaned, should be fastened in rows by a skewer, run through the heads, and then broiled and served hot.

A New System of Domestic Cookery, 1807

TO SERVE THORNBACK OR SKATE Should be hung one day at least, before it be dressed and may be served either boiled, or fried in crumbs, being first dipped in egg.

A New System of Domestic Cookery, 1807

TO BOIL TURBOT The turbot kettle must be of proper size and in the nicest order. Set the fish in cold water to cover it completely. Throw a handful of salt and one glass of vinegar into it; let it gradually boil. Be very careful that there fall no blacks, but skim it well, and preserve the beauty of the colour. Serve it garnished with a complete fringe of curled parsley, lemon and horseradish.

A New System of Domestic Cookery, 1807

TO DRESS TURTLE Kill it at night in the winter, and in the morning in summer. Hang it up by the hind fins, cut off the head and let it bleed well. Separate the bottom shell from the top, with great care, lest the gall bladder be broken; which must be cautiously taken out and thrown away.

Put the liver in a bowl of water. Empty the guts and lay them in water; if there be eggs, put them also in water. It is proper to have a separate bowl of water for each article.

Cut all the flesh from the bottom shell, and lay it in water; then break the shell in two, put it in a pot after having washed it clean; pour on as much water as will cover it entirely. Add one pound of middling, or flitch of bacon, with four onions chopped and set it on the fire to boil. Open the guts, cleanse them perfectly; take off the inside skin, and put them in the pot with the shell. Let them boil steadily for three hours, and if the water boils away too much add more.

Wash the top shell nicely after taking out the flesh, cover it, and set it by. Parboil the fins, clean them nicely, taking off all the black skin, and put them in water. Cut the flesh taken from the bottom and top shell, in small pieces. Cut the fins in two, lay them with the flesh in a dish; sprinkle some salt over and cover them up.

When the shell, etc., is done, take out the bacon, scrape the shell clean, and strain the liquor; which must be put back in the pot, about one quart of it. Reserve the rest for soup. Pick out the guts, and cut them in small pieces; take all the nice bits that were strained out, put them with the guts into the gravy. Lay in the fins cut in pieces with them and as much of the flesh as will be sufficient to fill the upper shell.

Add to it (if a large turtle) one bottle of white wine, cayenne pepper, and salt, to your taste; one gill of mushroom catsup, one gill of lemon pickle, mace, nutmeg, and cloves pounded, to season it high. Mix two large spoonfuls of flour in one pound and a quarter of butter. Put it in with thyme, parsley, marjoram and savory, tied in bunches. Stew all these together till the flesh and fins are tender.

Wash out the top shell; put a puff paste around the brim. Sprinkle over the shell pepper and salt, then take the herbs out of the stew; if the gravy is not thick enough, add a little more flour, and fill the shell. Should there be no eggs in the turtle, boil six new laid ones for ten minutes, put them in cold water a short time, peel them, cut them in two, and place them on the turtle. Make a rich forcemeat, fry the balls nicely, and put them also in the shell. Set it in a dripping pan, with something under the sides to keep it steady: have the oven heated as for bread, and let it remain in till nicely browned. Fry the liver, and send it in hot.

The Virginia Housewife, 1825

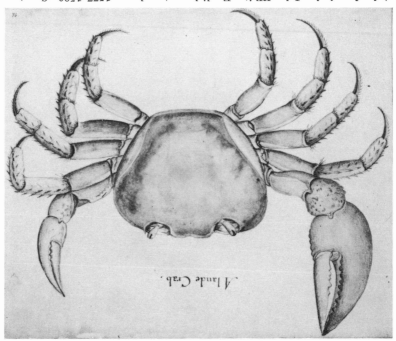

A land crab, by John White. English, watercolor, c. 1577–1590. *Courtesy Trustees of The British Museum.*

TO CURE TAINTED FISH Tainted fish may be much restored to its proper flavor by mixing a quantity of vinegar and salt in the water in which the fish is to be boiled.

The Family Receipt Book, 1819

TO MAKE A STRONG FISH GRAVY Take two or three eels, or any fish you have, skin or scale them, gut them and wash them from grit. Cut them into little pieces, put them into a sauce pan, cover them with water, a little crust of bread toasted brown, a blade or two of mace, some whole pepper, a few sweet herbs, and a little bit of lemon peel.

Let it boil till it is rich and good, then have ready a piece of butter, according to your gravy: if a pint, as big as a walnut. Melt it in the saucepan, then shake in a little flour, and toss it about till it is brown, and then strain in the gravy to it. Let it boil a few minutes and it will be good.

The Frugal Housewife, 1772

Carawayes; Spanish Potatoes; Virginia Potatoes; Potatoes of Canada, or Artichokes of Jerusalem, by John Parkinson. English, woodcut, 1629. *Courtesy The Garden Library, Dumbarton Oaks, Washington, D.C.*

Vegetables

One widely held Indian superstition predicted that a naked squaw strolling through her garden on a moonlit night and dragging her cloak behind her would prevent cutworms from destroying the vegetable crop. If true, Indian women during colonial times must have been marathon walkers, for corn, squash, pumpkins, beans, and peas grew abundantly throughout the colonies.

The Seneca tribe of the Iroquois Confederation had a romantic, if somewhat bizarre, explanation for the origins of the four major American vegetables. According to their beliefs, these foods sprang from the daughter of the holy Sky Woman, who in turn had descended from the heavens on the wings of birds. Soon after the daughter died and was buried in a shallow grave, corn sprang from her breast, squash plants grew from her abdomen, beans sprouted from her fingers, and potatoes from her toes. As an added benefit, tobacco grew from her head.

Although settlers seemed to reserve judgment on this explanation, vegetables soon became as vital to the survival of the colonists as to the lives of this country's red men.

Indian corn or maize was the most important food staple in the early settlement of America. Explorers from all sections of Europe seemed fascinated by the plant that grew so abundantly and required so little attention. Priests accompanying Hernando de Soto on his Florida expedition in the mid-1500s considered celebrating mass with corn bread, but rejected the idea as not befitting the dignity of the solemn ceremony. Maize, also called turkie wheat, was soon being tilled by English residents to the north. The plant was hardier than England's grains and flourished more readily in the weather and soil conditions of the new country.

A painted Indian woman of Florida, by John White. English, watercolor, c. 1577–1590. *Photo courtesy Library of Congress.*

Colonials followed many of the agricultural practices developed by Indians to cultivate their crops. Corn, pumpkins, and beans were planted together in the same fields at the same time. Early maturing stalks of corn were used as poles to support the climbing bean stems, while the ground vines of pumpkins helped to retain water and prevent erosion of the soil. One section of a field would be planted several weeks after the first, in order to extend the harvest season so that fresh vegetables would be available for a longer period.

Little day-to-day attention was needed to produce an adequate crop, but at certain critical times during the growing period, some precautions were taken. Because dead fish were used as fertilizer for the young plants, watch-men were needed to stand guard over newly planted fields to prevent wolves from digging up the decayed seafood. Eastern Indians also built large plat-forms in their fields to serve as lookout stations for spotting flocks of crows and other grain-eating birds capable of stripping recently sown fields in a single hour.

Colonists usually brought tools from the Old World, but homemade items were also a necessity. Metal-bladed hoes, shovels, harrows, mattocks, sickles, scythes, and dung forks were roughly produced on the farm and periodically refitted with wooden handles. Hand-tilling was widespread, for probably less than one-half of the farmers in colonial America owned plows. They also may have adopted various Indian implements, such as hoes made from clamshells, the shoulder bones of moose, and picks fashioned from deer antlers.

Generally, agricultural Indian tribes tended their crops more closely than did the newcomers from Europe. After the ground had been broken up and piled into small mounds by the entire tribe, women carefully planted and guarded the fields. Careful hoeing to remove weeds was constantly practiced. No fences separated the individual plots in an Indian field, but private owner-ship was sometimes recognized. The brave stealing another's crop was forced to work for the offended until the damage was repaid sufficiently in services.

After the crop was gathered, husking bees were gay celebrations in pioneer communities. Indians marked a successful harvest with an elaborate ceremony called the Green Corn Dance, which sometimes coincided with the Thanks-giving celebration of the Pilgrims or was held when the first kernels appeared on the cob.

During the autumn period, corn was eaten fresh, usually boiled or roasted on the cob. Another favorite harvest dish using the newly picked ears was a succotash stew of corn and beans. The name was probably adopted from sugut-tahhash, the most common Indian word for corn. Served Indian-style, the meal was occasionally flavored with diced dog meat and beans, a custom not adopted by Europeans, who substituted salt meat from less endearing animals. Although fresh corn mixed with meats and vegetables was prepared im-mediately after the harvest, the great majority of each year's crop was ground into meal for use during the winter and spring. Corn was never eaten primarily as a vegetable, but instead was a basic ingredient for porridges and breads. Following a plentiful autumn, Indians sacrificed the best kernels of the harvest to their gods and charred the remainder in open fires. Then it was

Indian women guarding the cornfields against crows, by Captain S. Eastman. American, engraving, 1853. *Photo courtesy Library of Congress.*

pounded into meal on a stone mortar or hollowed-out log. One product of this open-fire roasting was popcorn, which was then served with a topping of maple syrup. Pioneer housewives, however, reserved the best of the corn crop for the next year's planting, sun dried the kernels, and then used a mortar and pestle to grind it into coarse meal. As the colonies became more populated, gristmills began to be built and relieved the housewife of this time-consuming chore.

The American woman was particularly ingenious at inventing variations for what became a standard table item—corn pudding. The six most common recipes all involved meal and liquid, which were mixed in differing proportions and cooked various lengths of time. The most popular concoctions were:

—Hasty pudding, a quickly cooked gruel of cornmeal boiled in almost equal parts with milk or water. Hasty pudding was also called loblolly;

Indians planting maize, 1564. Engraving after Frenchman Jacques Le Moyne de Morgues, 1591. Photo courtesy Library of Congress.

—Indian pudding, a slightly more liquid version of hasty pudding which was boiled in a bag containing various spices;

—Suppawn, a thick mixture of cornmeal and milk, eaten either hot or cold from the pot, or allowed to cool. Then it could be also sliced and fried in deep fat;

—Mush, a watery type of suppawn eaten with sweetened fruit or molasses;

—Samp porridge, an Indian goulash featuring cornmeal cooked for a minimum of three days with meats and vegetables. After the prolonged simmering, this mixture became so thick that it could be removed from the pot in one solid chunk.

Cornmeal in its driest and most finely powdered form, however, was known on the frontier as rockahominy. Most travelers carried small bags of

1. *Milium Indicum maximum Maiz dictum five Frumentum Indicum vel Turcicum.* The usuall *Indian* or *Turkie* Wheate.

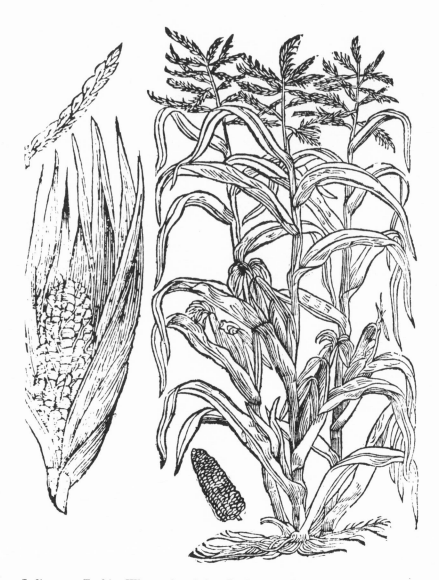

Indian or Turkie Wheat, by John Parkinson. English, woodcut, 1640.
Courtesy The Garden Library, Dumbarton Oaks, Washington, D.C.

this maize with them on the trail, and mixed the powder with water in the palm of their hands to get quick energy. A similar Indian trail dish was named nokik, perhaps meaning no cake or baked bread. This food of small weight was particularly nourishing, for during the early eighteenth century, it was estimated that a frontiersman could exist in the forest for half a year with only six pounds of rockahominy and two to four pounds of glue soup.

Hominy, hulled corn that was only partially ground, was sometimes preferred to fine meal in the South or in Scotch-Irish communities. Often this ''essence of corn'' was boiled and then topped with meat drippings for a main supper dish, or was fried and served with honey for breakfast. Indians, who called the coarse meal omene, boiled the corn with fish or eels and produced ''corn soop.''

Paintings of the first Thanksgiving invariably show giant pumpkins in places of prominence, for like corn this gourdlike food was a staple.

Both pumpkins and their cousin the squash grew luxuriously with little farming attention. Both foods were relatively unknown in the countries from which the new pioneers had come. American housewives, therefore, invented recipes on a trial and error basis, and early records show that these experiments were eaten with less than full enthusiasm in some cases.

Like corn, many pumpkin dishes were served with butter, sugared water, or molasses. Another variation was sweet pumpkin sauce, used as a topping on cornmeal mushes, thus preserving sugar for more important occasions. The still popular dish of baked pumpkin was originated by these early settlers who removed the pumpkin's core, baked the shell in cabbage leaves, and then served the whole vegetable with cream poured into the center.

Indians shared with pioneers various methods of drying and dicing this vegetable, which red men called pompions, so that the preserved chunks could be later reconstituted by boiling with other produce. Pumpkin pies and puddings could be prepared throughout the year, but because of the great abundance of fruits and berries, pumpkin filling was not considered the first choice for dessert. It was usually used only when other sweets were not available.

Squashes were prepared in many of the same ways as pumpkins, such as in boiled vegetable goulashes or puddings. In addition, they were often stewed with meats or candied with fresh fruits. One drawback, however, was the presence of tiny worms called ascarides, which bred in squashes and wreaked havoc on the gastrointestinal systems of many settlers.

Farmers also cultivated many varieties of both peas and beans. Indians

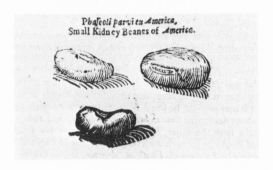

Small kidney beans of America, by John Parkinson. English, woodcut, 1640. *Courtesy The Garden Library, Dumbarton Oaks, Washington, D.C.*

had long grown both kidney and lima beans, and one American cookbook lists nine types of edible varieties cultivated during the period.

Beans were stewed, fricasseed, and pickled in an effort to provide interest to the everyday menu. But perhaps the most famous culinary creation was the standard Saturday night fare of New England baked beans or bean porridge. Indians probably originated this dish, for many tribes baked bean stews in earthen pots placed into pits and covered with hot ashes. For the colonial settler, the cooking process was slightly more refined.

In eighteenth-century Massachusetts, the large cooking ovens of taverns and inns served as communal-baking facilities for the entire community. Once a week, usually on Saturday, bean pots filled with raw ingredients would be carried to the inn from houses throughout the town. Individual recipes varied according to the household, but common to most were beans, molasses, salt, and meat fat. After the daylong baking was completed at the tavern, the bean pots were fetched home, usually by the children of each family.

In the South, field and green peas grew abundantly and were used more frequently than were beans. One seventeenth-century writer, assisting Lord Baltimore in his attempts to lure colonists to Maryland, insisted that the farmland was so fertile that peas grew a full ten inches in only ten days. While this may have been a slight exaggeration, peas were an important part of the southern diet.

Hoppin John, eaten by both the poorest farmer and the plantation owner, survives today as a special dish in South Carolina. In this mixture, black-eyed or field peas are cooked for several hours in water with onions and liberal amounts of salt pork. When nearly done, rice, salt, and pepper are added.

Pease porridge of nursery rhyme fame was common in Maryland and con-

1 Fabæ sativæ Garden Beanes. 2 Phaseoli sativi French Beanes. 3 Pisum vulgare Garden Peale. 4 Pisum umbellatum sive Rose Peale, Rose Peale or scottish Peale. 5 Pisum Saccharatum. Sugar Peale. 6 Pisum maculatum. Spotted Peale. 7 Cicer Arietinum. Rams Ciches or Ciccrs.

Garden Beans; French Beans; Garden Peas; Rose Pease; Sugar Peas; Spotted Peas; Rams Ciches or Ciccrs, by John Parkinson. English, woodcut, 1629. *Courtesy The Garden Library, Dumbarton Oaks, Washington, D.C.*

ower end, of a
riped, and as it
parts, where the
filberd kernell)
) another, being
rme and folide,
: fide, and white
ore oily.

Honorius Bellus,
:ne & Pulfe, unto
h in the defcrip-
the end of Sum-
from Lisbone by
aces of America
eof, both on the

refaid, to be the
za hath it) or τῶ
lis of Theophra-
eleaventh Chap-
:eeing fo rightly
ruit groweth as
ing to the fmall
re faith alfo, that
r any thing like
a fence and rea
doe fufpect the
to himfelfe, for
r ground than a-
: above ground,
fee not, for I ne-
: bore fruit above
: comparifon un-
ibilitie : but fure-
athered the rootes with the fruit on them when the ftalkes and leaves were
e plant, as it is likely, or gathering it himfelfe : the etimologie alfo of the
δ'ιον, Aracus and hudnon, which is tuber, confirmeth a fuppofail in me, that
like the fruit of the foregoing Aracus above ground, and fuch like is the un-

1, 2, 3. *Arachidna Cretica Honorij Belli: Sub terra fili-
quifera Lufitanica, & Americana magna.*
Vnder ground Peafe or Cichelings of Candy, Portugall,
and a great kinde of *america.*

Underground peas, by John Parkin-
son. English, woodcut, 1640. *Courtesy
The Garden Library, Dumbarton Oaks,
Washington, D.C.*

sisted of a cooked pea mush, which had been sieved and flavored with spices,
pepper, and butter. A similar dish in New York involved several different
types of peas cooked with butter, celery, and ginger. Pea plants provided Indians with a wide assortment of treats, for not only was the pea itself eaten,
but also the plant's stalks, shoots, leaves, and pods.

Sweet potatoes may have been first imported into America from Brazil via
Spain and Florida; however, some writers suggest that this vegetable was
indigenous to the Deep South. Regardless of origin, by the eighteenth century
this starchy food flourished as far north as Delaware. Slaves from the West
Indies and Africa created succulent new methods for preparing sweet potatoes,
which formed an intricate part of their own food rations.

Sweet potatoes, a member of the morning glory family, were mixed with

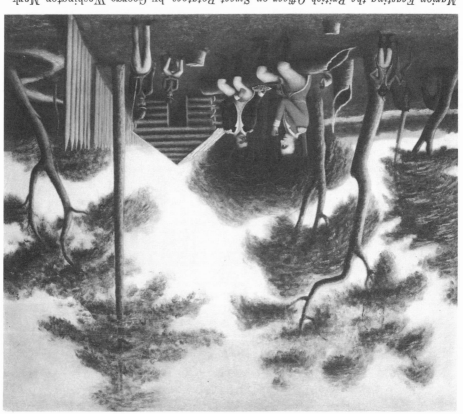

Marion Feasting the British Officer on Sweet Potatoes, by George Washington Mark. American, oil on canvas, 1848. Courtesy National Gallery of Art, Washington, D.C., gift of Edgar William and Bernice Chrysler Garbisch.

molasses and nuts for puddings, roasted over open fires, or made into flat pancakes. One special stew called for halved potatoes to be covered with slices of smoked ham, which in turn was topped with cut up chickens and stewed for many hours. "A dainty and costly dish for the table," described by one seventeenth-century writer, was made from sweet potatoes baked with marrow, sugar, and spices.

The history of the white or Irish potato is also conflicting. They may have been native to North America, but several experts believe they were first sent from Peru to Spain and then brought to Florida in the sixteenth century by the conquistadores.

Seventeenth-century Europeans called them potatoes of Virginia or apples of youth, but to the pioneers the vegetable was not so sweet. Early settlers believed that eating the white potato would bring certain death in seven years and thus prepared it only in times of near starvation when death was even more imminent. The plants, however, were shipped back to England where they quickly became popular as a cheap, easily produced staple. Years later, white potatoes were brought back to the colonies by Irish settlers and thus derived the name Irish potatoes.

Potatoes and milk were often the simple breakfast of farm families, but the vegetable was also prepared as a main dinner entree. In one recipe, the potato was smothered under a mixture of butter, sugar, dates, mace, grape juice, cinnamon, nutmeg, and pepper. Potatoes were also fried, mashed, and stewed as a vegetable side dish much as they are served today.

Rice was first introduced into America about 1680 from Madagascar. In South Carolina and the Georgia low country, rice fields tended by ever increasing numbers of African slaves flourished and rice soon became a major export to the North. This versatile grain was usually served as a vegetable, but was also mixed with French barley in soups. Pilaf, or rice slowly simmered in meat broth, was a favorite dish in the two most southern colonies. Shrimp and okra were also added to rice to produce a type of gumbo.

Ground rice was used instead of wheat flour in making bread, and it was a lucky household that enjoyed a special dish of boiled rice with small wild

Rice, by John Parkinson. English, woodcut, 1640. *Courtesy The Garden Library, Dumbarton Oaks, Washington, D.C.*

oranges. At breakfast, rice was mixed with milk as a beverage, boiled into a thick water pudding, or toasted into waffles.

Jerusalem artichokes, so called because the bottom of the plant is shaped similarly to the heart of an artichoke, were also known as the potatoes of Canada. Exotic discoveries from the colonies were often greeted with great excitement in Europe, but quickly lost their allure after adaptation to Old World soil. The Jerusalem artichoke is a good example of this fall from glamour.

In 1629, British horticulturalist John Parkinson wrote: "'The potato's of Canada are by reason of their great increasing, growne to be so common here with us at London, that even the most vulgar begin to despise them, whereas when they were first received among us, they were dainties for a Queene.''

Although the most common vegetables consumed were corn, pumpkin, squash, beans, potatoes, and rice, a wide variety of other foods was available to the colonists by the mid-seventeenth century. Since the climate of the northern colonies was similar to that of Britain, many of the vegetables that had first been imported were soon flourishing in local gardens alongside domestic plants that had been cultivated by the Indians.

Meats were stewed with cabbages, parsnips, and carrots. Also available were artichokes, beets, cauliflower, asparagus, turnips, spinach, endive, a type of parsnip called skirrets, and colewort, a variety of cabbage.

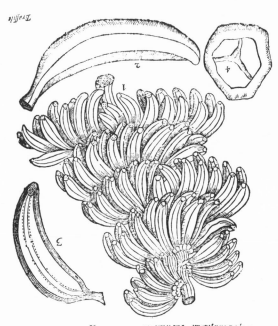

Musa's bruyfru'm. The fruite of the said Indian Figge or Plantaine tree.

Trujillo

The Indian Fig or Plantaine Tree, by John Parkinson. English, woodcut, 1640. Courtesy The Garden Library, Dumbarton Oaks, Washington, D.C.

Skirrits; Parsneps; Carrets; Turneps; Navewes; Blacke Raddish; Common Raddish, by John Parkinson. English, woodcut, 1629. *Courtesy The Garden Library, Dumbarton Oaks, Washington, D.C.*

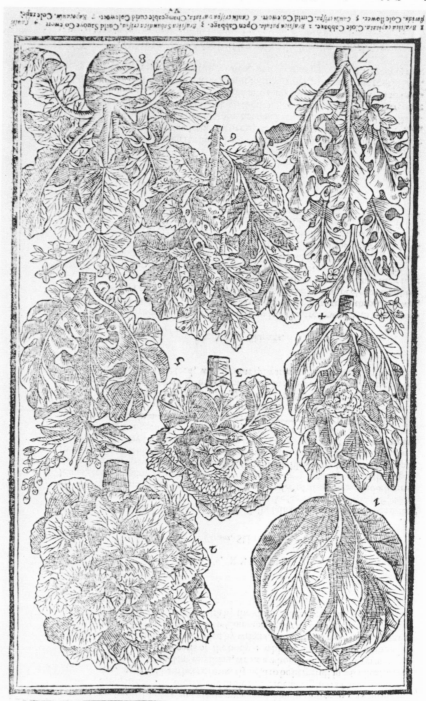

Close Cabbage; Open Cabbage; Curld Sauoye Colewort; Cole Flower; Curld Cole-wort; Changeable curld Colewort; Cole rape, by John Parkinson. English, woodcut, 1629. Courtesy The Garden Library, Dumbarton Oaks, Washington, D.C.

South Carolinians cooked with tomatoes as early as 1710, but these "love apples" were not widely eaten until one hundred years later. Although it was native to South America, the tomato, like the potato, was probably introduced into the northern continent by European immigrants.

Wild onions were eaten raw, used in flavoring stews, and were roasted. Some, however, were saved for times of illness when it was believed that a slice or two was a sure cure for measles.

The profuseness with which life-sustaining vegetables grew in the colonies was memorialized by Plymouth's Governor William Bradford, a poet who evidently did not believe in brief titles for his works. Bradford lists many of America's abundant vegetables in his seventeenth-century poem entitled "Some Observations of God's Mercifull Dealing with us in this Wildernesse and His Gracious Protection over us These Many Years, Blessed be His Name."

The poem, in part, explains:

> All sorts of roots and herbs in gardens grow,
> Parsnips, carrots, turnips, or what you'll sow,
> Onions, melons, cucumbers, radishes,
> Skirrets, beets, coleworts, and fair cabbages . . .
> Nuts and grapes of several sorts here are,
> If you will take the pains them to seek for . . .

Mixed greens and vegetable salads, topped with oil and vinegar dressings, were well known to the colonists. Wild greens, such as leeks, pigweed, cowslip, cress, milkweed, ferns, purslane, swamp cabbage, and the leaves of the pokeberry bush, were often eaten raw in a dish called sallet. In some cases, these were supplemented with radishes, violets, sorrel, sunflowers, spinach, savory, wild rhubarb, mushrooms, endive, and turnip greens. Beet tops, dandelions, and lettuce were all important salad greens. Cucumbers, believed valuable in unstopping the liver, were also used in salads.

A favorite salad prepared by housewives in old New York was a mixture of thinly shredded cabbage and vinegar. The dish, called koolslaa, was a forerunner of modern cole slaw.

Fish salads, made from greens mixed with onions and pieces of shellfish topped with oil and vinegar, are recorded as having been eaten in colonial Virginia, while in the same colony, some early adventurers managed to survive after consuming salads of jimson or Jamestown weed. This hardy plant has since proven to be highly poisonous, causing blindness or death.

While meat was the major foodstuff of most white colonists, vegetables and grains probably formed the bulk of the diet of American slaves.

Food allotments for blacks varied according to the financial means of the slave owner, but weekly rations in southern areas universally included corn-meal, sweet potatoes, seasonal vegetables, and rice. Specified allotments of each commodity were given to each working slave with fractional amounts provided for children. The amount of rations in some cases may have also depended upon the types of work being performed by the slaves, with larger proportions sometimes given to field gangs who were engaged in manual labor, than to artisans or house servants.

The early 1712 South Carolina slave code prohibited any slave from raising corn, peas, and rice, but in practice many plantation owners probably provided small private plots near the slave quarters where black workers were expected to raise vegetables to supplement their basic weekly rations. This gardening was done during the slaves' time off, which was usually on

Athore and Laudonnière at Ribault's Column, 1564. Engraving after Frenchman Jacques Le Moyne de Morgues, 1591. Florida Indians, worshiping a column set up by French explorers, have brought offerings of food. *Photo courtesy Library of Congress.*

Sundays, holidays, or late in the afternoon after many hours of work in the plantation fields had been completed.

Peas and turnips were raised for cooking in vegetable stews, which also included small amounts of salt pork, bacon, dried fish, or wild game if available. Other vegetables were grown, but usually only those that required little attention.

Laws regulating farming were coupled with statutes forbidding the sale or barter of any produce by slaves. These regulations were partially to protect the market prices of small farmers who could easily be undersold by slave-produced items. The laws were also designed to discourage slaves from stealing produce grown by the plantation owner and selling it as his own. The most significant exceptions were in port towns such as Savannah where seamen slaves bartered freely for produce, liquor, or fruit.

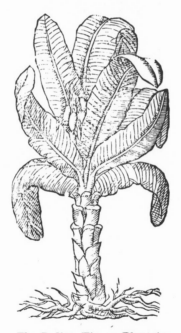

The Indian Fig or Plantaine Tree, by John Parkinson. English, woodcut, 1640. *Courtesy The Garden Library, Dumbarton Oaks, Washington, D.C.*

Vegetable Recipes

TO COOK JERUSALEM ARTICHOKES Must be taken up the moment they are done, or they will be too soft. They may be boiled plain, or served with white fricassee sauce.

The American Domestic Cookery, 1822

TO PICKLE ASPARAGUS First put your asparagus in a glazed earthen pot, then pour upon it water boiling hot, mixed with salt, then let it be closed up in a pot, and kept fast covered. But when you use them they must be taken out two hours before and laid in cold water. Then boil them and let melted butter be put to them and they will be fit to be sent to the table.

New American Cookery, 1805

TO PRESERVE BUSH BEANS FRESH AND GOOD TILL WINTER Take half a bushel of beans of a suitable size and age for eating green. String and break them, then put them into a cask, first sprinkling in salt, then a laying of beans, and so alternately till the cask is full, then add a weak brine so as to cover them. Take out for use, and freshen twenty four hours in water, often changing it : boil three hours in fresh water.

New American Cookery, 1805

TO BOIL FRESH BEANS Take your beans and string them, cut in two and then across. When you have done them all, sprinkle them over with salt, stir them together, as soon as your water boils, put them in and make them boil up quickly. They will be soon done and they will look of a better green than when growing in the garden. If they are very young, only break off the ends ; then break in two and dress them in the same manner.

The New England Cookery, 1808

TO PICKLE CABBAGES   Provide two quarts of vinegar with some mace, and two ounces of pepper. Put it on the fire and when it has boiled about ten minutes, cut the cabbages into thin slices, and pour it upon them in earthen pots, which must be tied up and corked to prevent the air from getting in, and your pickle will be fit for use in ten days.

New American Cookery, 1805

TO COOK CARROTS   Carrots require a good deal of boiling. When young, wipe off the skin after they are boiled; when old, boil them with the salt meat and scrape them first.

The American Domestic Cookery, 1822

TO BOIL CAULIFLOWERS   Choose those that are close and white. Cut off the green leaves; and look carefully that there are no caterpillars about the stalk. Soak an hour in cold water: then boil them in milk and water; and take care to skim the sauce pan, that not the least foulness may fall on the flowers. It must be served very white, and rather crisp.

The American Domestic Cookery, 1822

TO FRY CELERY   Take six or eight heads of celery, cut off the green tops, and take off the outside stalks. Wash them clean; then have ready half a pint of white wine, the yolks of three eggs beat fine, and a little salt and nutmeg. Mix all well together with flour, into a batter. Dip every head into the batter, and fry them in butter. When enough, lay them in the dish and put melted butter over them.

The Frugal Housewife, 1772

TO CURE MUSTY CORN   Immerse it in boiling water; let it remain till the water becomes cold. The quantity of water should be at least double the quantity of corn to be purified.

The Husbandman and Housewife, 1820

TO MAKE INDIAN CORN PUDDING Three pints scalded milk, seven spoons fine Indian meal. Stir well together while hot. Let stand till cooled; add seven eggs, half pound raisins, four ounces butter, spice and sugar. Bake one and half hours.

or

Salt a pint of meal, wet with one quart milk, sweeten and put into a strong cloth, brass or bell metal vessel, stone or earthenware pot, secure from wet, and boil twelve hours.

American Cookery, 1796

ANOTHER INDIAN PUDDING Three pints scalded milk to one pint meal salted. Cool, add two eggs, four ounces butter, sugar or molasses and spice. It will require two and one half hours baking.

The New England Cookery, 1808

TO STEW CUCUMBERS Pare twelve cucumbers and slice them as for eating and put them to drain, and lay them in a coarse cloth till they are dry. Flour them, and fry them brown in butter. Then put to them some gravy, a little claret, some pepper, cloves and mace and let them stew a little. Then roll a bit of butter in flour, and toss them up. Put them under mutton and lamb roasted.

The Compleat Housewife, 1730

TO MAKE GUMBO A West Indian Dish. Gather young pods of ochra, wash them clean and put them in a pan with a little water, salt and pepper. Stew them till tender, and serve them with melted butter. They are very nutritious and easy of digestion.

The Virginia Housewife, 1825

TO MAKE SCOTCH LEEK SOUP Put the boiling of a leg of mutton into a stew pot, with a quantity of chopped leeks, and salt. Simmer them an hour, then mix some oatmeal with a little cold water quite smooth. Pour it into the soup and setting it on a slow part of the fire, let it simmer gently, but take care that it does not burn to the bottom.

A New System of Domestic Cookery, 1807

TO COOK SEA KALE   Is tied up in bundles and dressed in the same way as asparagus.

The Virginia Housewife, 1825

TO STEW MUSHROOMS   The large buttons are best, and the small flaps while the fur is still red. Rub the large buttons with salt and a bit of flannel; cut out the fur and take off the skin from the others. Sprinkle them with salt, and put into a stew pan with some pepper-corns. Simmer slowly till done; then put a small bit of butter and flour, and two spoonfuls of cream. Give them one boil and serve with sippets of bread.

The American Domestic Cookery, 1822

TO MAKE AN EXCELLENT CATSUP WHICH WILL KEEP GOOD MORE THAN TWENTY YEARS   Take two gallons of stale strong beer, or ale, the stronger and staler the better. One pound of anchovies, cleansed from the intestines and washed. Half an ounce each of cloves and mace, one quarter do. of pepper, six large roots of ginger; one pound of eschalots and two quarts or more of flap mushrooms well rubbed and picked.

Boil these ingredients over a slow fire for one hour. Then strain the liquor through a flannel bag, and let stand till quite cold when it must be bottled and stopped very close with cork and bladder, or leather. One spoonful of this catsup to a pint of melted butter, gives an admirable taste and color, as a fish sauce, and is by many preferred to Indian soy.

The Universal Receipt Book, 1814

TO MAKE MUSH   Put a lump of butter the size of an egg into a quart of water. Make it sufficiently thick with corn meal and a little salt; it must be mixed perfectly smooth. Stir it constantly till done enough.

The Virginia Housewife, 1825

TO MAKE OCHRA SOUP   Get two double handfuls of young ochra, wash and slice it thin, add two onions chopped fine, put it into a gallon of water at a very early hour in an earthen pipkin, or very nice iron pot. It must be kept steadily simmering but not boiling : put in pepper and salt.

At twelve o'clock, put in a handful of lima beans ; at half passed one o'clock, add three cimlins cleaned and cut into small pieces, a fowl, or knuckle of veal, a bit of bacon or pork that has been boiled and six tomatoes, with skin taken off. When nearly done, thicken with a spoonful of butter ; mixed with one of flour. Have rice boiled to eat with it.

The Virginia Housewife, 1825

TO ROAST ONIONS   Should be done with all the skins on. They eat well alone, with salt only, and cold butter ; or with roast potatoes, or with beetroots.

A New System of Domestic Cookery, 1807

TO PRESERVE PARSLEY FRESH AND GREEN   To garnish viands in winter. Put any quantity of green parsley into a strong pickle of salt and water boiling hot, and keep for use.

New American Cookery, 1805

TO FRICASSEE PARSNIPS   Boil in milk till they are soft. Then cut them lengthways into bits two or three inches long ; and simmer in a white sauce made of two spoonfuls of broth, a bit of mace, half a cupful of cream, a bit of butter, and some flour, pepper and salt.

The American Domestic Cookery, 1822

TO STEW PARSNIPS   Boil them till tender, scrape them from the dirt, cut them into slices, put them into a sauce pan, with cream enough for sauce, a piece of butter rolled in flour, a little salt, and shake the sauce pan often. When cream boils, pour them into a plate for a corner-dish or a side dish at supper.

The Frugal Housewife, 1772

TO BOIL GREEN PEAS   When your peas are shelled and the water boils which should not be much more than will cover them, put them in with a few leaves of mint, as soon as they boil put in a piece of butter as big as a walnut, and stir them about. When they are done enough, strain them off, sprinkle in a little salt, shake them till the water drains off, send them hot to the table with melted butter in a cup or boat.

American Cookery, 1796

PEAS PORRIDGE OR SOOP   Take two gallons of peas and boil them in a little water, till they are very thick and soft enough to strain. Then strain them. Take some knuckles of veal and a leg of mutton; prick it well with a knife to let out the gravy, and boil it in as much water as will cover it. When all the goodness is boiled out of the meat strain it and put it into the pulp of the peas, and boil them together very well.

Put in a good store of sparement, and a little thime, and some bacon if you please. When it is boiled enough, have some rashers of bacon ready fried to lay round the top of the dish, and put in a great deal of butter and serve it to the table.

The Family Dictionary, 1705

TO KEEP GREEN PEAS TILL CHRISTMAS   Take young peas, shell them, put them in a colander to drain, then lay a cloth four or five times double on a table. Then spread them on, dry them very well, and have your bottles ready. Fill them, cover them with mutton suet fat when it is a little soft; fill the necks almost to the top, cork them, tie a bladder and a leather over them and set them in a dry cool place.

American Cookery, 1796

TO BOIL POTATOES   Parboil, then slice and broil them; or parboil, and set them whole on the gridiron over a very slow fire; and when thoroughly done, send up with their skins on. The latter is done in many Irish families.

A New System of Domestic Cookery, 1807

TO MAKE POTATOE BALLS Mix mashed potatoes with the yolk of an egg, roll them into balls, flour them, or cover them with egg and bread crumbs. Fry them in clean drippings, or brown them in a Dutch oven. They are an agreeable vegetable relish or a supper dish.

The Virginia Housewife, 1825

TO FRY POTATOES Cut them into thin slices, as big as a crown piece. Fry them brown, lay them in the plate or dish. Pour melted butter and sack and sugar over them.

The Frugal Housewife, 1772

TO BROIL SWEET POTATOES Cut them across without peeling, in slices half an inch thick. Broil them on a griddle, and serve them with butter in a boat.

The Virginia Housewife, 1825

TO STEW SWEET POTATOES Wash and wipe them, and if they be large, cut them in two lengths. Put them at the bottom of a stew pan, lay over some slices of boiled ham, and on that one or two chickens cut up with pepper, salt and a bundle of herbs. Pour in some water and stew them till done. Then take out the herbs, serve the stew in a deep dish—thicken the gravy and pour over it.

The Virginia Housewife, 1825

TO MAKE PUMPKIN PUDDING One quart milk, one pint pumpkin, four eggs, molasses, allspice and ginger, in a crust, bake one hour.

American Cookery, 1796

TO FIX PUMPKIN SEEDS Afford an oil with the greatest facility and abundance. One gallon of seeds it is said will yield about half a gallon of oil. They may be pressed like grape seed or flax seed. The oil is clear, limpid, pale and scentless and when used for sallet instead of sweet oil has merely a faint insipid taste : it burns well and without smoke.

The Husbandman and Housewife, 1820

TO MAKE SAVORY RICE Wash and pick some rice. Stew it very gently in a small quantity of veal or rich mutton broth, with an onion, a blade of mace, pepper and salt. When swelled, but not boiled to mash, dry it on the shallow end of a sieve, before the fire, and either serve it dry, or put it in the middle of a dish, and pour the gravy round, having heated it.

A New System of Domestic Cookery, 1807

TO COOK BUTTERED RICE Prepare some rice as above: drain and put it with some new milk, enough just to swell it, over the fire. When tender, pour off the milk, and add a bit of butter, a little sugar, and pounded cinnamon. Shake it that it do not burn and serve.

A New System of Domestic Cookery, 1807

TO MAKE A DISH OF RICE TO BE SERVED UP WITH THE CURRY IN A DISH BY ITSELF Take half a pound of rice, wash it clean in salt and water. Then put it into two quarts of boiling water, and boil it briskly twenty minutes. Strain it through a colander and shake it into a dish, but do not touch it with your fingers nor with a spoon.

Beef, veal, mutton, rabbits, fish, etc. may be curried and sent to the table with or without the dish of rice.

Curry powder is used as a fine flavored seasoning for fish, fowl, steaks, chops, veal cutlets, hashes, minces, a-la-modes, turtle soup, and in all rich dishes, gravies, sauces, etc., etc.

The Virginia Housewife, 1825

TO MAKE RICE SOUP To two quarts of water, put three quarters of a pound of rice, clean picked and washed, with a stick of cinnamon; let it be covered very close, and simmer till your rice is tender; take out the cinnamon, and grate half a nutmeg; beat up the yolks of four eggs and strain them to half a pint of white wine, and as much pounded sugar as will make it palatable. Put this to your soup, and stir it till it boils, and is of a good thickness; then send it to the table.

The New England Cookery, 1808

TO PREPARE SALLADS FOR WINTER   Take a good hard cabbage, and with a sharp knife shave it so thin you may not discern what it is, then serve it with oil and vinegar. Or take corn sallad clean picked and also well washed, clear from the water, put it in a dish in some handsome form, with some horseradish scraped and some oil and vinegar.

The Family Dictionary, 1705

TO MAKE SKIRRET FRITTERS   Take a pint of pulp of skirrets, and a spoonful of flour, the yolks of four eggs, sugar and spice, make it into a thick batter, and fry them quick.

The Art of Cookery, 1747

TO STEW SPINACH AND EGGS   Pick and wash your spinach very clean, put it into a sauce pan without water, throw in a little salt, cover it close, and shake the pan often. When it is just tender, and whilst it is green, put it into a sieve to drain, and lay it in your dish.

In the meantime have a stew pan of water boiling, break as many eggs in separate cups as you would poach. When the water boils, put in the eggs; have an egg-slice ready to take them out with, lay them on the spinach, and garnish the dish with orange cut up in quarters and send up melted butter in a cup.

New American Cookery, 1805

TO COOK SQUASH OR CIMLIN   Gather young squashes, peel and cut them in two. Take out the seeds, and boil them till tender. Put them into a colander, drain off the water, and rub them with a wooden spoon through the colander. Then put them into a stew pan, with a cup full of cream, a small piece of butter, some pepper and salt—stew them stirring very frequently until dry. This is the most delicate way of preparing squashes.

The Virginia Housewife, 1825

TO MAKE A CROOKNECK OR WINTER SQUASH PUDDING   Core, boil and skin a good squash, and bruise it well; take six large apples, pared, cored and stewed tender, mix together; add six or seven spoonfuls of dry bread or biscuit, rendered fine as meal, half pint milk or cream, two spoons of rose water, two do. wine, five or six eggs beaten and strained; nutmeg, salt, and sugar to your taste, one spoon flour, beat all smartly together, bake.

The above is a good receipt for pumpkins, potatoes or yams, adding more moistening or milk and rose water, and to the two latter a few black or Lisbon currents or dry whortleberries scattered in will make it better.

American Cookery, 1796

WINTER SQUASH   The crooked neck of this squash is the best part. Cut it in slices an inch thick, take off the rind and boil them with salt in the water; drain them before they are dished and pour melted butter over. Serve them up very hot.

The large part containing the seeds, must be sliced and pared—cut it in small pieces and stew it till soft, with just enough water to cover it. Pass it through a sieve and stew it again, adding some butter, pepper, and salt. It must be dry, but not burnt. It is excellent when stewed with pork chops.

The Virginia Housewife, 1825

TO BAKE TOMATOES   Cut some tomatoes in two the broad way, put them up on a tin, with the part where there is rind downwards; strew up on each a seasoning of pepper, salt and sweet herbs chopped small. Set them into an oven till they are soft, and serve them up without any other sauce.

The American Domestic Cookery, 1822

TO MAKE TOMATO CATSUP   Gather a peck of tomatoes, pick out the stems and wash them. Put them on the fire without water, sprinkle on a few spoonfuls of salt, let them boil steadily an hour, stirring them frequently. Strain them through a colander, and then through a sieve. Put the liquid on the fire with half a pint of chopped onions, half a quarter of an ounce of mace, broke into small pieces, and if not sufficiently salt, add a little more—one tablespoon of whole black pepper; boil all together until just enough to fill two bottles; cork it tight—make it in August in dry weather.

The Virginia Housewife, 1825

TO MAKE TOMATO OR LOVE APPLE SAUCE   Take the ripest and best tomatoes, carefully strip them of their outer peel, and cut out the insertion of the stalk and any spots which may be upon them.

Divide them in eight parts or slices, and take out a part, if not the whole of the seeds. Put them into a sauce pan, or even spider, with a very little butter previously melted, and cover them close, in order to keep in the steam.

When nearly done, add to them salt and pepper to taste, and replacing the cover, let them stand a little longer. Should it be desirable to thin the sauce, add a little water to it just before it is done.

The Universal Receipt Book, 1814

TO MAKE VEGETABLE SOUP   Pare and slice five or six cucumbers, the inside of as many cos lettuces, a sprig or two of mint; two or three onions, some pepper and salt, a pint and a half of young peas, and a little parsley. Put these with a half a pound of fresh butter, into a sauce pan to stew in their own liquor near a gentle fire half an hour; then pour two quarts of boiling water to the vegetables, and steam them two hours. Rub down a little flour into a teacup of water; boil it with the rest fifteen or twenty minutes and serve it.

A New System of Domestic Cookery, 1807

Nova Virginiae Tabvla. Holland, hand-colored engraving, 1606. *Courtesy Colonial Williamsburg, Williamsburg, Virginia.*

Fruits & Nuts

Long before Englishmen had set foot on American soil, Spanish settlers in Florida successfully cultivated tasty fruits in their gardens. Saint Augustine's sixteenth-century plots provided a wide assortment of both imported and indigenous fruit, including figs, guavas, pomegranates, grapes, lemons, limes, citrons, and mandarin oranges. Later, plantains, a banana-type fruit, and the shaddock also became part of Spain's contribution to the food repertoire of the New World.

In the North, one of the first projects of English pioneers was the planting of fruit trees. Soon after settlers had constructed their rough cabins, men of the family set to work clearing fields for fruit orchards.

Apples were particularly favored for they supplied the necessary ingredients for the hundreds of gallons of cider and applejack that every pioneer family consumed each year. One problem, however, was wild bear, which took an instant liking to the sweet red fruit and broke many young branches while climbing the trees in search of juicy morsels.

Not all of the fruit was reserved for liquor. Beside the cider jugs on the colonial hearth, dried apple strings hung ready for use in cooking pies and tarts. Spiced apple butter and apple sauce provided condiments to be served with porridge and fish, while baked apples, marmalades, and jellies topped the canning lists of early American women.

Peaches, also introduced into Florida by the Spanish adventurers, were soon grown as far north as Pennsylvania, and hung so heavily on the trees that about 1630 one owner of a small hog farm claimed to have fed at least one hundred bushels to his swine in a single season. In the Deep South, corn whiskey was liberally poured over peaches as a method of preservation. This

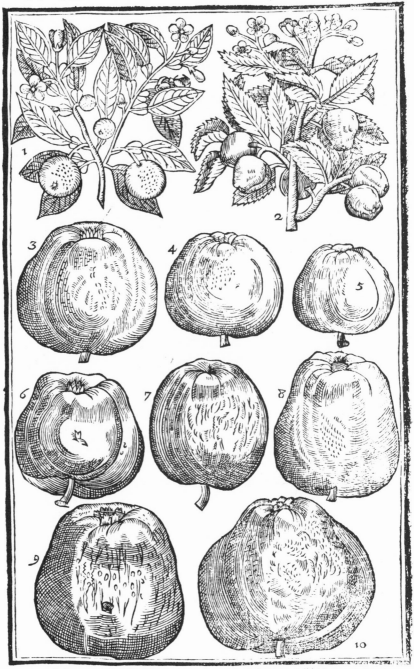

The Orenge tree; The Apple tree; The Pomewater; The golden Pippin; The Pearemaine; The Queene Apple; The Genneting; The pound Royall; The Kentish Codlin; The Bardfield Quiuing, by John Parkinson. English, woodcut, 1629. *Courtesy The Garden Library, Dumbarton Oaks, Washington, D.C.*

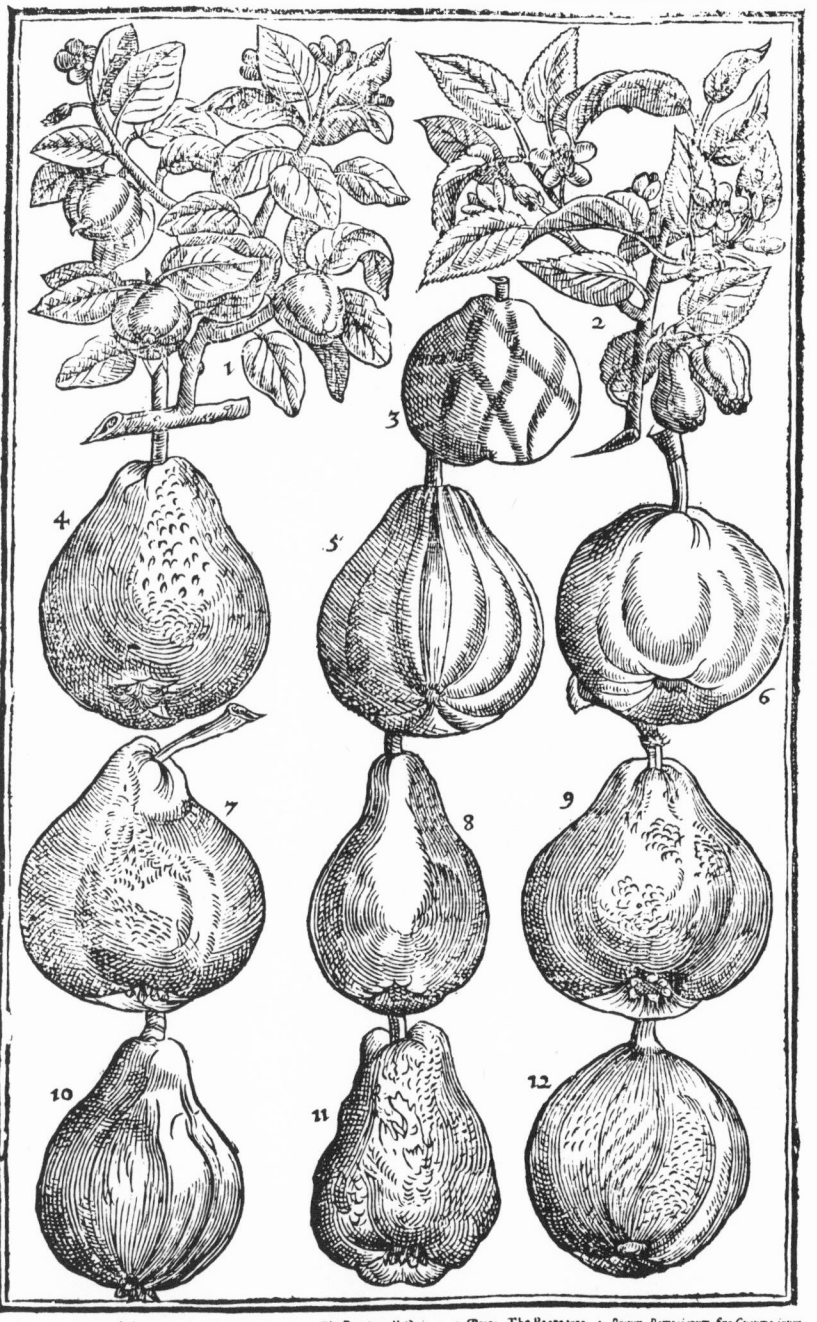

The Quince tree; The Portiagall Quince; The Peare tree; The Winter Bon Chretien; The painted or striped Peare of Jerusalem; The Burgomot Peare; The Summer Bon Chretien; The best Warden; The pound Peare; The Windsor Peare; The
Gratiola Peare; The Gilloflower Peare, by John Parkinson. English, woodcut, 1629.
Courtesy The Garden Library, Dumbarton Oaks, Washington, D.C.

The Pomecitron Tree, by John Parkinson. English, woodcut, 1640. *Courtesy The Garden Library, Dumbarton
Oaks, Washington, D.C.*

interesting technique helped to account for the great popularity of peaches
in the southern colonies.

Spring in the forest provided the colonists with an assortment of wild
berries, such as huckleberries, whortleberries, cranberries, gooseberries, raspberries, blackberries, boxberries, gingerberries, checkerberries, blueberries, and
strawberries. The freshly picked fruits were eaten much as they are today
with cream and sugar, or baked into pies. One particularly popular fresh
berry dish was a baked pudding of fresh cranberries, flour, and molasses. The
cranberry was unknown in Europe before the settlement of the colonies, and
early settlers named the plants bearberries, because eastern bears so frequently
fed on the fruit.

There is no record that indicates fresh fruits and berries were eaten as
salads. Because the fresh food season was so short, most berries were sugared or
otherwise preserved for future use.

Berries were dried, pounded into a hard paste, and then cut into squares
which were chewed like candy. All types of fruits were preserved whole with
sugar and then reconstituted many months later for pie filling or tarts. Berry

paste in dough cases was a Thanksgiving tradition, while puréed fruit supplied the major flavoring in scores of dessert creams. Chopped fruits were boiled with syrup or sugar to produce marmalades and jellies that could be spread on toast or biscuits. One old New England recipe for sowens requires that oatmeal be soured in water and then boiled with fruit jelly or fresh figs.

Wild elderberries, mulberries, and grapes were used for wine-making, and other alcoholic drinks were produced from pears, peaches, currants, and shrub roots. The native persimmon was brewed into a light beer, which was popular not only with European settlers but with Indians. Wild plums for Christmas puddings were almost a necessity in English immigrant homes.

Small wild oranges and lemons were originally shipped north from Florida and Georgia, but were later replaced by more tasty domestic citrus fruits from Barbados. A dish with something of a kick was prepared by Florida Indians who scooped out the tops of wild oranges, filled the inside with honey, and allowed the mixture to ferment.

Several great mansions built in the seventeenth and eighteenth centuries reflect the efforts of mid-Atlantic colonists to produce homegrown tropical fruit. An integral part of these buildings was a large glass-paned structure called an orangery. Here it was hoped the northern settler would be able to grow his own tropical fruit indoors and eliminate the expense of importation.

The Indian Hony Plumme or Mango, by John Parkinson. English, woodcut, 1640. Courtesy The Garden Library, Dumbarton Oaks, Washington, D.C.

Some of these efforts were successful. A 1751 entry in the diary of John Blair of Williamsburg details a trip to a nearby plantation where fresh oranges were gathered.

Quinces, currants, persimmons, apricots, and cherries were available to be eaten raw or in dessert dishes as was the custom of the period. One of the most popular fruit dishes was the native muskmelon, which had long been planted by agricultural Indians in the eastern seaboard section. The larger water-melon was also a favorite, particularly in the southern colonies.

Soon more exotic foods such as maracock or passion fruit were being grown, and tropical products not suited to the country's climate were available on an imported basis. One early recipe attempted to satisfy those settlers who could not afford expensive imported items by describing how to make an imitation mango out of a watermelon or cucumber. Mango was a term applied not only to a specific tropical plant, but to any pickled melon.

Tree nuts and buds also served as important sources of food. Acorns were staples of most Indian tribes who extracted great quantities of oil from the buds. Because these seeds are poisonous in their natural state, the red men devised elaborate bleaching and boiling processes to ensure safety in eating and storage. Pinecones, also called pineapples, were much in demand as basic flavoring ingredients in marchpane candy, pastries, and other confectionaries. Not only was the taste desired, but the cone supposedly possessed medicinal qualities that were good for the lungs and a sore throat.

The products of other trees such as chestnuts, filberts, walnuts, and hickory nuts were also choice items. They were considered valuable not only as spices, but when ground into flour were used in making bread. Hazelnuts were frequently fed to the sick as a stimulant to the appetite.

Nuts were pickled, served as snacks, or used in stuffing. One recipe for "forcing" game birds called for ground chestnuts to be mixed with fowl's liver, ground ham, parsley, mace, nutmeg, pepper, and salt. Another use for chestnuts and also for hickory nuts was found by Indians who boiled the nuts with corn for several hours. The result was a nourishing milk substitute used in cooking.

The ground or earth nut is frequently mentioned as a food staple that was eaten baked and buttered. The modern identity of this plant is uncertain, but it may have been the nutlike root of a wild pea plant. Groundnuts were well known in Europe under the name of chinaroot.

Nuts were also used as the basic ingredient in catsups, a liquid of great

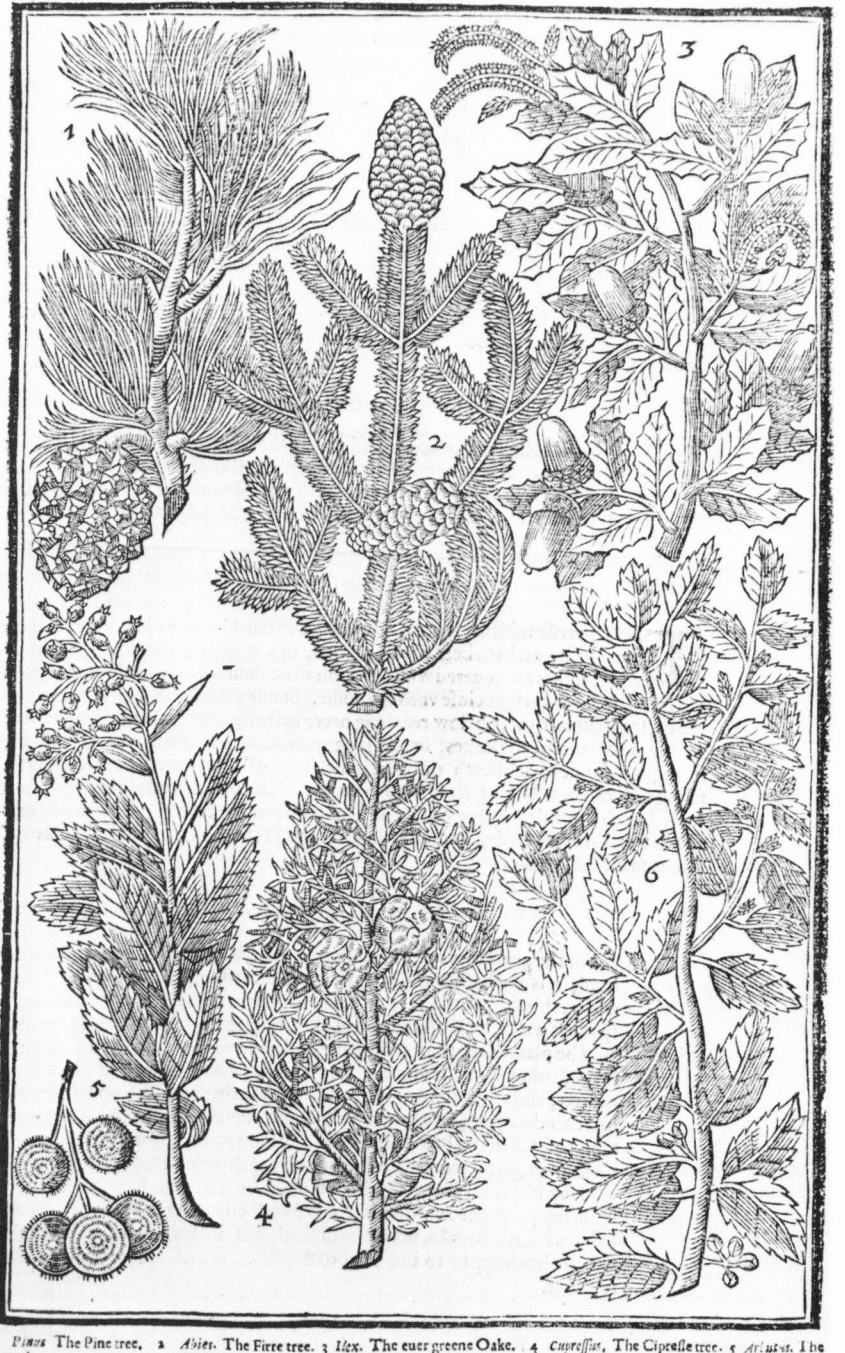

x *Pinus* The Pine tree. 2 *Abies.* The Firre tree. 3 *Ilex.* The euer greene Oake. 4 *Cupressus*, The Cipresse tree. 5 *Arbutus.* The Strawberry tree. 6 *Alaternus.* The euer greene Priuer.

Ees

The Pine tree; The Firre tree; The euer greene Oake; The Cipresse tree; The Strawberry tree; The euer greene Priuer, by John Parkinson. English, woodcut, 1629. *Courtesy The Garden Library, Dumbarton Oaks, Washington, D.C.*

importance in American kitchens. Unlike today's hamburger sauces of the same name, colonial catsups did not necessarily require a tomato base. Walnut catsup, a mixture of boiled vinegar, spices, and pounded nuts, was particularly popular. These liquid relishes, which were bottled and preserved for many years, were primarily used in flavoring meat and vegetable dishes as they were being cooked.

Basket of Fruit, by Mary Bradley. American, painting on velvet, c. 1830. *Courtesy Abby Aldrich Rockefeller Folk Art Collection, Williamsburg, Virginia.*

Fruit and Nut Recipes

TO MAKE BLACK CAPS Halve and core some fine large apples; put them in a shallow pan: strew white sugar over, and bake them. Boil a glass of wine, the same of water, and sweeten it for sauce.

A New System of Domestic Cookery, 1807

TO MAKE MARMALADE OF APRICOCKS Gather your apricocks just turn'd from the green of a very pale yellow. Pare them thin and weigh them, three quarters of a pound of double refined sugar to a pound of apricocks. Then cut them in halves, take out the stones and slice them thin. Beat your sugar and put it in your preserving pan with your sliced apricocks and three or four spoonfuls of water. Boil and scum them, and when they are tender put them in glasses.

The Compleat Housewife, 1730

A CURIOUS AND SIMPLE MANNER OF KEEPING APRICOTS, PEACHES, PLUMS, ETC. FRESH ALL THE YEAR Beat well up together equal quantities of honey and spring water; pour it into an earthen vessel. Put in the fruits all freshly gathered and cover them up quite close. When any of the fruit is taken out, wash it in cold water, and it is fit for immediate use.

The Universal Receipt Book, 1814

TO PRESERVE CHERRIES Take two pounds of cherries, one pound and a half of sugar, half a pint of fair water. Melt some sugar in it; when it is melted, put in your other sugar and your cherries. Then boil them softly till all the sugar be melted. Then boil them fast and skin them. Take them off two or three times and shake them, and put them on again and let them boil fast and when they are of a good colour, and the syrup will stand, they are boiled enough.

American Cookery, 1796

TO MAKE AMERICAN CITRON Take the rine of a large watermelon not too ripe. Cut it into small pieces, take two pounds of loaf sugar, one pint of water, put it all into a kettle, let it boil gently for four hours, then put it into pots for use.

American Cookery, 1796

A MODE OF PICKLING MELONS OR CUCUMBERS SO AS TO IMI-TATE REAL MANGOES Cut a square piece out of the sides of the melons or cucumbers, and take out the seeds with a teaspoon. Put the fruit into very strong salt and water for a week, stirring them well two or three times a day. Then place them in a pan, on a good quantity of vine (or cabbage) leaves, and cover them over with as many more. Beat fine a little roche alum, put it into the salt and water, out of which the melons have been taken, pour it over them and set them on a very slow fire for four or five hours or till they get a good green.

Take them out, drain them in a hair sieve, and when cold, fill into them horseradish, mustard seed, garlic, and pepper corns. If the fruit be cucumbers, put a few slices of cucumbers in the center of this mixed stuffing. Sew on with thread the pieces taken out, and to every gallon of vinegar for covering and preserving them add an ounce each of mace and cloves; two ounces each of allspice, sliced ginger root and long and black pepper; two ounces of garlic; a large stick of horseradish; and three ounces of mustard seed tied up in a bag.

Boil this well together for a few minutes only; and pouring it on the pickles, close up the jar air-tight. The confinement of the mustard seed in a bag, is a very good method to adopt on other occasions.

The Universal Receipt Book, 1814

TO KEEP ORANGES AND LEMONS Take small sand and make it very dry; after it is cold, put a quantity of it into a clean vessel; then take your oranges and set a laying of them in the sand, the stalk end downwards, so that they do not touch each other, and strew in some of the sand, as much as will cover them two inches deep; then set your vessel in a cold place, and you will find your fruit high preservation at the end of several months.

The Family Receipt Book, 1819

TO DRY PEACHES Take the fairest and ripest peaches, pare them into fair water: take their weight in double refined sugar. Of one half make a very thin syrup; then put in your peaches, boiling them till they look clear, then split and stone them.

Boil them till they are very tender, lay them a-draining, take the other half of the sugar, and boil it almost to a candy. Then put in your peaches, and let them lie all night. Then lay them on a glass, and set them in a stove till they are dry. If they are sugar'd too much, wipe them with a wet cloth a little : let the first syrup be very thin, a quart of water to a pound of sugar.

The Frugal Housewife, 1772

TO MAKE SYRUP OF PEACH BLOSSOMS Infuse peach blossoms in hot water, as much as will handsomely cover them. Let them stand in balneo, or in sand, for twenty-four hours covered close. Then strain out the flowers from the liquor, and put in fresh flowers. Let them stand to infuse as before, then strain them out, and to the liquor put fresh peach blossoms the third time, and if you please, a fourth time.

Then to every pound of your infusion, add two pounds double refined sugar, and setting it in sand or balneo, make a syrup, which keep for use.

The Art of Cookery, 1747

TO STEW PEARS Pare six pears, and either quarter them or do them whole : they make a pretty dish with one whole, the rest cut in quarters, and the cores taken out. Lay them in a deep earthen pot, with a few cloves, a piece of lemon peel, a gill of red wine, and a quarter of a pound of fine sugar.

If the pears are very large, they will take half a pound of sugar, and a half a pint of red wine; cover them close with brown paper, and bake them till they are enough.

Serve them up hot or cold, just as you like them, and they will be very good with water in the place of wine.

The Frugal Housewife, 1772

TO MAKE PEAR MARMALADE   Boil the pears till soft—when cold, rub the pulp through a sieve and boil it into a jelly, allowing one pound of sugar to two of pears.

The Virginia Housewife, 1825

TO MAKE PLUM PORRIDGE OR BARLEY GRUEL   Take a gallon of water, half a pound of barley, a quarter of a pound of raisins clean washed, a quarter of a pound of currants cleaned, washed and picked. Boil these till above half the water is wasted, with two or three blades of mace. Then sweeten it to your palate and add half a pint of white wine.

The Art of Cookery, 1747

TO PRESERVE PLUMS   Take your plums before they have stones in them, which you may know by putting a pin through them. Then caudle them in many waters till they are as green as grass, peel them and caudle them again. You must take the weight of them in sugar, a pint of water, then put them in, set them on the fire to boil slowly till they be clear, skimming them often, and they will be very green. Put them up in glasses and keep them for use.

American Cookery, 1796

TO MAKE MARMALADE   To two pounds of quinces put three quarters of a pound of sugar and a pint of spring water. Then put them over the fire, and boil them til they are tender; then take them up and bruise them; then put them into the liquor, let it boil three quarters of an hour, and then put it into your pots or sauces.

The Frugal Housewife, 1772

TO PRESERVE STRAWBERRIES   Get the largest strawberries before they are too ripe. Have the best loaf sugar, one pound to each of strawberries —stew them very gently, taking them out to cool frequently, that they may not be mashed : when they look clear, they are done enough.

The Virginia Housewife, 1825

TO CANDY ANY SORT OF FRUIT After you have preserved your fruit, dip them suddenly into warm water to take off the syrup; then sift on them double-refined sugar till they look white; then set them on a sieve in a warm oven, taking them out to turn two or three times. Let them not be cold till they be dry and they will look clear as diamonds. So keep them dry.

The Compleat Housewife, 1730

TO FRICASY ALMONDS Take a pound of Jordan almonds; do not blanch them, or but one half of them; beat the white of an egg very well and pour it on your almonds, and wet them all over. Then take half a pound of double refined sugar, and boil it to sugar again; and put your almonds in and stir them till as much sugar hangs on them as will.

Then set them on plates, and put them into the oven to dry after bread is drawn, and let them stay in all night. They will keep the year round if you keep them dry, and they are a pretty sweetmeat.

The Compleat Housewife, 1730

TO MAKE WALNUT CATSUP Gather the walnuts as for pickling, and keep them in salt and water the same time. Then pound them in a marble mortar—to every dozen walnuts put a quart of vinegar: stir them well every day for a week, then put them in a bag and press all the liquor through. To each quart put a teaspoon of pounded cloves, and one of mace, with six cloves of garlic. Boil it fifteen or twenty minutes and bottle it.

The Virginia Housewife, 1825

TO PICKLE WALNUTS Take walnuts about midsummer, when a pin will pass through them, and put them in a deep pot, and cover them with ordinary vinegar. Change them into fresh vinegar once in fourteen days, till six weeks be past; then take two gallons of the best vinegar and put into it coriander-seeds, carraway-seeds, dill-seeds, of each an ounce grossly bruised, ginger sliced three ounces, whole mace one ounce, nutmeg bruised two ounces, pepper bruised two ounces, give all a boil or two over the fire, and have your nuts ready in a pot, and pour the liquor boiling hot over them; so do for nine times.

The Compleat Housewife, 1730

Captain BUN Quixote attacking
the OVEN.

Pu' according to Act Jan.] 4.ᵈ 1773 by Darly 39 Strand.

Captain Bun Quixote Attacking the Oven. English, 1773. *Courtesy Colonial Williamsburg, Williamsburg, Virginia.*

Breads

The first recorded menu for a Thanksgiving celebration indicates that both white and corn breads were part of the banquet fare at Plymouth Colony. Fifty years later, Christmas breads baked by Germans in the mid-Atlantic colonies were carefully frozen as future remedies for the winter fevers that were sure to beset the entire family.

But bread in colonial America was not reserved only for special holidays, such as Thanksgiving and Christmas. It was manna in the true sense of every-day nourishment and an important part of the diet.

Settlers assured themselves of a ready supply of bread grains by carefully cultivating the wheat, barley, oats, and rye seeds brought to the new country on immigrant ships. Millet, long grown by local Indians, was also planted and like the other common grains was known under the collective name of corn.

The fertile earth of the New World produced record crops for even the most inexperienced farmer. Dutch settlers in New Netherlands found that they could sow wheat for as long as eleven years without replenishing the rich soil, and this inexpensive grain quickly became a common table item. Wheat also was a leading crop, particularly in Pennsylvania, and together with rye was exported to Georgia and the Carolinas at a large profit to the growers.

Practices such as annual planting of fields soon leached the once fertile soil and reduced the original record crops. In many areas, the per acre harvest of the American farmer fell far short of his counterpart in Europe. The reasons are many, but primarily the colonial settler was not a full-time farmer. Equally important to his survival were hunting, housing construction, tool manufacture, and other basic tasks of new settlement, which were largely

Ark of the Covenant, by Erastus Salisbury Field. American, oil on canvas, c. 1865–1880. *Courtesy National Gallery of Art, Washington, D.C.; gift of Edgar William and Bernice Chrysler Garbisch.*

absent in Europe. This left little time for extensive weeding, gleaning, and pruning. Unlike the Old World where fields had been cleared for centuries, the colonial farmer was forced to fell hundreds of virgin trees if he was to have a second field for rotating his crops. Cross-plowing to aerate the soil was time-consuming, even if a plow and team could be borrowed.

In times when the supply of finer grains ran low, settlers found substitutes for the traditional breads. The results are recipes that are uniquely American, such as the various cornmeal mixtures. In the South, both ground rice and dried pumpkin were often baked into biscuits along with the ever plentiful potato which, when dried and pounded, produced flour used in the preparation of muffins and fritters.

Captain John Smith described a particularly high protein bread invented by Virginia adventurers out of desperation during a famine. The once elegant

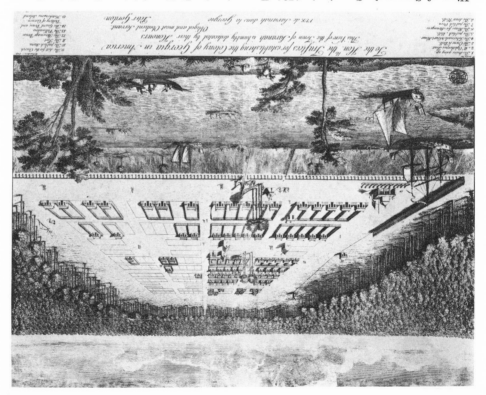

View of Savannah, Georgia, in 1734. Engraving by P. Fouhdrinier after Peter Gordon. Photo courtesy *Library of Congress.*

cavaliers, deprived of the more desirable grains, mixed dried sturgeon, caviar, sorrel, and herbs to produce bread.

Breads were eaten at all meals, but were particularly popular at break-fast. The colonist's day traditionally began with a mug of cider and some sort of cake, the early name for any small flatbread that was baked on the fireplace hearth.

Corn cakes were universal favorites at any meal. The ingredients and pro-portions varied in each section of the country, but generally this most American of all breads included one part liquid, three parts Indian meal, and one-half part flour. In the North, these cakes made with scalded milk were called johnnycakes or journeycakes because they remained fresh throughout long trips. In other regions, boiling water was substituted for milk and meat drippings were added to the batter.

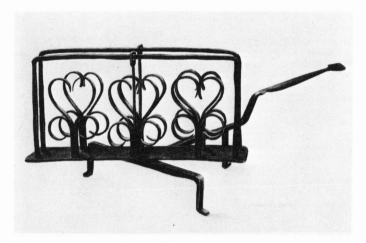

Iron toast rack with rotating bread holder. American. *Courtesy National Gallery of Art, Index of American Design.*

Eighteenth-century American waffle iron. *Courtesy National Gallery of Art, Index of American Design.*

In the South, some corn breads were called hoecakes, because they were usually baked inside a fireplace on the flat end of a hoe. Hoecakes were popular with field slaves who could cook the hot breads on their work tools laid near bonfires in the open fields.

Citizens in prerevolutionary days lived simple, unadorned lives, and thus many of the names of early foods are derived directly from the ingredients or methods of preparation.

Ashcakes were made from cornmeal, grease, and water, which was mixed, wrapped in cabbage leaves, and then cooked Indian fashion among the smoldering fireplace logs. Scratch backs were prepared from a thick corn pudding that became hard and uneven on top after cooking, thus scratching the back of the diner's mouth when eaten.

Bannock cake was baked on a bannock board, and the famous Maryland beaten biscuits were so called because the dough was beaten with a heavy ax handle for at least one hour before cooking. Hoecake batter dripped from a spoon into deep fat became corn dabs, because of their small size. But, perhaps the most descriptive of all was rye and injun, a hard bread made from cornmeal and rye to be carried on the trail while hunting.

Wheat flour was a basic ingredient not only for loaf breads, but in biscuits, muffins, and a special toasted sweet bread called rusk. Seedcakes, or tumbles, also required finely ground flour, along with sugar, butter, eggs, and caraway seeds. The mixture was thoroughly beaten or tumbled together.

Stale or leftover breads were not thrown away, but served as valuable ingredients in the production of other dishes such as bread fritters. In this dish, slices of bread were flavored with wine, dipped into beaten eggs, and fried to a golden brown in lard. Bread when soaked with pureed onion and milk and boiled into a mush became a meat sauce.

Southern settlers may have enjoyed coontie bread, a staple of Floridian Indians. Roots from the zamia and smilax plants were pounded and mixed with water. The liquid was then stirred and poured into a jar where the flour settled to the bottom. Finally the water was poured off, the flour dried and baked. To the North, Indians made similar breads from pounded tuckahoe and groundnut roots. Pones prepared from wheat and hominy were common dishes among agricultural tribes who varied the recipe with different types of nut flour.

Although yeast was brought to America by the early settlers, light risen breads did not become everyday items until just prior to the Revolution. Most yeasts were homemade from potatoes, with the sour cultures being passed from family to family and from generation to generation. Most leavened loaves of white breads were present only on special occasions. The wealthy planter, though able to import fine British yeasts, probably substituted local short-breads or biscuits for English crumpets with his afternoon tea.

Breads before the early 1700s were usually not the light, mild-tasting treats we enjoy today. Because importation costs made sugar and spices beyond the reach of many, molasses was often used as a sweetening. Butter was also a rare commodity before milk became popular around 1700. Churns were considered a luxury item until the mid-eighteenth century, and most butter was obtained by tedious hand-shaking of a large wooden bowl. After an arm-tiring period, small amounts of butter finally formed.

Most shortening requirements were satisfied by suet, lard, or meat drippings, which easily became rancid without refrigeration. Water or wine replaced cream in recipes, and if yeast was not available, settlers used emptins or emptyings from the bottom of beer barrels. Other substitutes were potash or pearl ash, compounds that supposedly gave a lightness to breads. Most often, however, artificial ingredients were not used, and light bread was produced by long beating of the dough or by the addition of egg whites.

This trial and error mixing of bread ingredients was not tolerated in many communities where bread was sold to the public. In Massachusetts, both the quality and quantity of bread was regulated by the General Court. Bakers attempting to sell substandard loaves were subject to fines for violating these early consumer protection laws.

The introduction of the long-handled waffle iron could have tempted many a colonial housewife to splurge her pantry of butter, cream, and sugar. The basic recipes for waffles required many of the ingredients that were most precious in the colonial kitchen, such as numerous eggs, heavy cream, wines, spices, and fine wheat flour.

Cookielike wafers were baked in similar griddle irons, but were prepared from a thinner batter with sugar and nuts added as extra treats. Long-handled skillets also allowed the early housewife to prepare dark buckwheat cakes, which were usually eaten with melted butter and milk. White flour pancakes were also popular, with some recipes calling for wine flavoring.

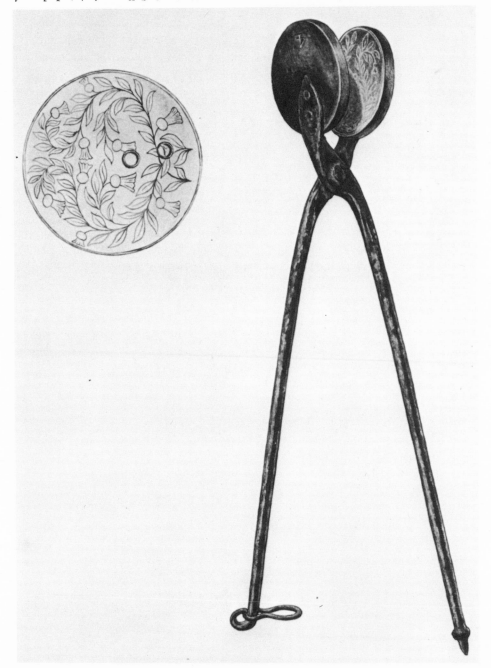

Eighteenth-century American wafer iron. Courtesy National Gallery of Art, Index of American Design.

Bread Recipes

BISCUITS

TO MAKE BISCUIT   One pound flour, two ounces butter, one egg, wet with milk and break while the oven is heating and in the same proportion.

New American Cookery, 1805

TO MAKE DROP BISCUIT   Beat eight eggs very light, add to them twelve ounces of flour, and one pound of sugar. When perfectly light, drop them on tin sheets and bake them in a quick oven.

The Virginia Housewife, 1825

TO PREPARE TEA BISCUIT   Two pounds flour, two spoons yeast in a little warm milk, mix them together, adding one quarter of a pound melted butter with milk, to make it into a stiff paste. Bake in a quick oven, in any shape you please.

New American Cookery, 1805

BREAD

TO COOK BREAD FRITTERS   Cut your bread of a convenient size—pour on it some white wine and let it stand a few minutes. Drain it on a sieve, beat four eggs very light, add four spoonfuls of wine. Beat all well together. Have your lard boiling. Dip the bread in the egg and fry it a light brown; sprinkle sugar on each and glaze them.

The Virginia Housewife, 1825

TO PREPARE BREAD SAUCE Boil a large onion, cut into four, with some black peppers and milk till the onion is quite a pap. Pour the milk strained on grated white stale bread, and cover it. In an hour, put it into a sauce pan, with a good piece of butter mixed with a little flour. Boil the whole together and serve.

The American Domestic Cookery, 1823

TO BAKE CORN MEAL BREAD Rub a piece of butter the size of an egg into a pint of corn meal. Make it a batter with two eggs and some new milk. Add a spoonful of yeast. Set it by the fire an hour to rise. Butter little pans and bake it.

The Virginia Housewife, 1825

TO MIX DIET BREAD One pound sugar, nine eggs, beat for an hour. Add to fourteen ounces flour, spoonful rose water, one do. cinnamon or coriander, bake quick.

American Cookery, 1796

A GOOD MIXED BREAD Put a teaspoon of salt and a large one of yeast into a quart of flour. Make it sufficiently soft with corn meal gruel. When well risen, bake it in a mould. It is an excellent bread for breakfast. Indifferent flour will rise much better, when made with gruel than with fair water.

The Virginia Housewife, 1825

TO MAKE ARTIFICIAL OR POTATOE BREAD Put a pound of potatoes in a net, into a skillet with cold water and (lest the skin break, and let in the water) hang it at a distance (so as not to boil) over the fire till they become soft. Then skin, mash and rub them so as to be well mixed with a pound of flour, a very large spoonful of salt, and two large spoonfuls of yeast; but less of the yeast is better.

Then add a little warm water, and knead it up as other dough; lay it a little while before the fire to ferment or rise; then bake it in a very hot oven.

Bread made in this manner has been frequently tried and found to be well-tasted, wholesome and of good conscience.

The Family Receipt Book, 1819

TO MAKE RICE BREAD   Boil six ounces of rice in a quart of water till it is dry and soft. Put it into two pounds of flour, mix it well; add two teaspoons of salt, two large spoonfuls of yeast and as much water as will make it the consistence of bread; when well risen, bake it in the molds.

The Virginia Housewife, 1825

TO MAKE WHITE BREAD AFTER THE LONDON WAY   You must take a bushel of the finest flour well dressed, put it in the kneading-trough at one end ready to mix. Take a gallon of water (which we call liquor) and some yeast. Stir it into the liquor till it looks of a good brown colour and begins to curdle, strain it and mix it with your flour, till it is about the thickness of a good seed cake. Then cover it up with the lid of the trough, and let it stand three hours, and as soon as you see it begin to fall, take a gallon more of liquor, and weigh three quarters of a pound of salt, and with your hand, mix it well with water.

Strain it and with this liquor make your dough of a moderate thickness fit to make up into loaves. Then cover it again with the lid and let it stand three hours more. In the meantime, put the wood into the oven and heat it. It will take two hours heating. When your spurge has stood its proper time, clear the oven and begin to make your bread. Set it in the oven and close it up, and three hours will just bake it. When once it is in you must not open the oven till the bread is baked; and observe in the summer that your water be milk warm, and in winter as hot as you can have your finger in it.

The Art of Cooking, 1747

CORN CAKES

TO MAKE JOHNNY CAKE OR HOE CAKE   Scald one pint of milk and put to three pints of Indian meal and half pint of flour. Bake before the fire.

or

Scald with milk two thirds of the Indian meal or wet two thirds with boiling water, add salt, molasses and shortening. Work up with cold water pretty stiff and bake as above.

The New England Cookery, 1808

TO MAKE INDIAN SLAPJACKS One quart of milk, one pint of Indian meal, four eggs, four spoons of flour, little fat, beat together, bake on griddles or fry in dry pan, or bake in a pan which has been rubbed with suet, lard or butter.

American Cookery, 1796

PANCAKES

TO MAKE BATTER CAKES Boil two cups of small hominy very soft, add an equal quantity of corn meal with a little salt, and a large spoonful of butter; make it in a thin batter with three eggs, and a sufficient quantity of milk—beat all together some time, and bake them on a griddle, or in waffle irons. When eggs cannot be procured, yeast makes a good substitute. Put a spoonful in the batter, and let it stand an hour to rise.

The Virginia Housewife, 1825

TO COOK BUCKWHEAT CAKES One quart buckwheat flour, one pint of milk or new beer, three spoons molasses, four do. yeast, stir well together, wet the bottom of the pan with butter or lard, and when the pan is hot, put in the cakes. When done, pour over butter and milk.

New American Cookery, 1805

TO MAKE PANCAKES Take a pint of thick cream, six spoonfuls of sack and half a pint of flour, six eggs (but only three whites) one grated nutmeg, a quarter of a pound of melted butter, a very little fat, some sugar; fry these thin in a dry pan.

The Frugal Housewife, 1772

PANCAKES TO MAKE CRISP Make twelve or twenty of them in a little frying pan, no bigger than a saucer, then boil them in lard and they will look yellow as gold, and eat very well.

The Family Dictionary, 1705

PASTRIES

PASTRY FOR TARTS Take two pounds and a half of butter, to three pounds of flour, and a half a pound of fine sugar beaten; rub all your butter in the flour, and make it into a paste with cold milk, and two spoonfuls of brandy.

PASTRY FOR PUFF PASTE Take a quartern of flour, and a pound and a half of butter; rub a third part of the butter in flour; and make a paste with water. Then roll out your paste, and put your butter upon it in bits, and flour it. Then fold it up and roll it again. Then put in more butter, and flour it, and fold it up again; then put the rest of the butter in, flour it, fold it and roll it twice before you use it.

PASTRY FOR RAISED PIES To half a peck of flour, take two pounds of butter, and put it in pieces in a sauce pan of water over the fire, and when the butter is melted, make a hole in the flour, skimming off the butter, and put it in the flour, with some of the water; then make it up in a stiff paste, and put it before the fire in a cloth, if you do not use it presently.

The Frugal Housewife, 1772

SWEET BREADS

TO MAKE MUFFINS Mix two pounds of flour with two eggs, two ounces of butter melted in a pint of milk, and four or five spoonfuls of yeast. Beat it thoroughly and set it to rise two or three hours. Bake on a hot hearth in flat cakes. When done on one side turn them.

A New System of Domestic Cookery, 1807

TO MAKE RUSK Rub in half a pound sugar, half a pound butter, to four pounds flour, add a pint milk, pint emptins; when risen well, bake in pans ten minutes, fast.

New American Cookery, 1805

TO MAKE EMPTINS Take a handful of hops and about three quarts water, let it boil about fifteen minutes, then make a thickening as you do for starch, which add when hot. Strain the liquor, when cold, put a little emptins to work it; it will keep in the bottle well corked five or six weeks.

New American Cookery, 1805

TO BAKE SWEET POTATO BUNS Boil and mash a potato, rub into it as much flour as will make it like bread, add spice and sugar to your taste, with a spoonful of yeast; when it has risen well, work in a piece of butter; bake in small rolls to be eaten hot with butter, either for breakfast or tea.

The Virginia Housewife, 1825

TO MAKE TUMBLES Three pounds flour, two pounds sugar, one pound butter and eight eggs, with a little carraway seed; bake on tins; add a little milk if the eggs are not sufficient.

New American Cookery, 1805

TO MAKE WAFERS One pound flour, quarter pound butter, two eggs, beat; one glass wine and nutmeg to make it palatable.

New American Cookery, 1805

WAFERS TO MAKE Take a quart of flour heaped, and put to it the yolks of four eggs, and two or three spoonfuls of rosewater, mingle this well together; then make it like batter, with cream and a little sugar and bake it on irons, very thin poured on.

The Family Dictionary, 1705

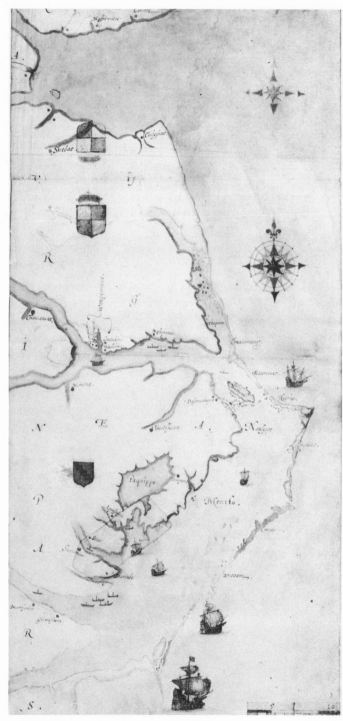

Map of North America From Florida to Chesapeake Bay, by
John White. English, watercolor, c. 1577–1590. *Courtesy Trustees
of the British Museum.*

Desserts

As sugar and syrups became more plentiful, confectioneries began to replace fresh or preserved fruit as the chief satisfiers of the settler's sweet tooth.

Flummery and syllabub are two picturesque names, largely forgotten today, but prominent in their time. Unlike the more basic puddings and custards, these two dishes were usually on the menus of the more aristocratic colonial families.

Flummery was a soft cream custard, thickened by gelatin from the marrow of a boiled calf's foot, then topped with an assortment of ground nuts, syrups, and fruit preserves. A less costly variation was made from oatmeal soaked for forty-eight hours in water and then boiled. The dish was served with sugar, cider, wine, or milk on top. Syllabub involved a complicated process of curdling cream with lemon, adding wine and sugar, and finally whipping the mixture to a stiff froth.

Simpler, nonalcoholic desserts called creams were flavored with pureed fruits or berries and chopped nuts. The same sieved fruit, when mixed with custard instead of whipped cream, became known as a fool. During the winter in the North, or in southern areas where ice was shipped in to cool beverages, dishes of dessert creams were set into containers of chilled water. The result was the forerunner of ice cream.

Early cooks concocted tasty puddings not only from fruits, but from mashed vegetables such as carrots, rice, pumpkin, corn, or sweet potatoes. Boiled flour pudding was perhaps the least costly of all afterdinner dishes. Also on the favored list were whitspots, or bread puddings baked in pastry shells.

Colonials feasted on wild berry or fruit pies and tarts as early as 1640. The popular legend that George Washington's cook invented apple pie during the general's stay at Valley Forge is indeed patriotic but not accurate. Pies were important parts of the evening supper meal, but were so well liked in New England that they became a breakfast tradition. Pies with no top crust were known as trap pies, while those with pastry on all sides were aptly named coffin pies.

Deep-dish cobblers became established desserts, for they could be cooked in the same heavy iron pots that were used in preparing stews and required no special equipment. The scooped-out boards called trenchers, which were the plates of most pioneers, reflected the American fondness for pie. After the main meal had been eaten, the trenchers were turned upside down, revealing a clean bottom nicknamed the pie side. The dessert course was served on this surface, free from the remains of the main meal.

Cakes were made long before the Revolutionary War with the most prominent being fruit, cheese, and spice cakes. Also a favorite was the pound cake, so named because it required a pound each of butter, sugar, eggs, and flour. Gingerbread cake, made with thick dark molasses, was a poorer class solution to the problem of high sugar prices.

With the frugality that marked cooking in most homes, stale cake was set aside for future use in the making of other desserts. For example, beg-

Ceramic pie plate with serrated edge dredged from the Chesapeake Bay. American, c. 1760. *Courtesy The Smithsonian Institution.*

gars' pudding included mounds of stale bread or cake mixed with currants, nuts, spices, and wines. Trifles required several layers of stale cake, soaked in brandy, and then spread with jam and whipped cream.

Sweetmeats was a term widely applied to any dessert-type dish, but specifically referred to a mixture of chopped fruits candied with nutmeats. These could be eaten at any meal of the day and were sometimes highly flavored with brandy. In Dutch settlements, sweetmeats were especially popular not only as a separate dish but as a sauce for puddings and creams.

Candies were also important in colonial times. Dried sweetmeats such as candied lemon peel were known as suckets, and, as the name implies, were sucked like hard rock candy. The roots and seeds of various plants, when dried and coated with sugar, became comfit candy. The choicest comfit treats were produced from almonds, coriander, caraway, and angelica.

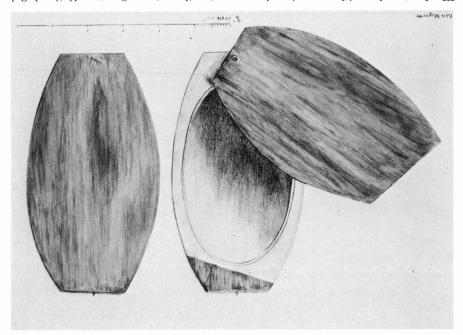

Wooden trencher with cover. American, seventeenth century. *Courtesy National Gallery of Art, Index of American Design.*

Simple mixtures of sugar boiled with water and flavored with some spice were probably the typical candy of most American families. Molasses and horehound sweets were particularly favored because of the inexpensive ingredients and the ease of preparation. Peppermint drops, a simple combination of sugar, egg whites, and peppermint flavoring, were also available. Candied flowers took their place along with roots and seeds as sweet tidbits on the colonial table.

On the more exotic side, confectioneries with mysterious names such as Salem Gibraltars and blackjacks were imported from Europe for sale. Marzipan, a mixture of nutmeats, sugar, and whipped egg whites, was traditional in Dutch New York.

Although the first American cheese factory was not established until 1851, various types of homemade cheeses were prepared throughout the colonies from the earliest days. In 1632, immigrants from Europe were warned that rennet, a cheese activate, should be included in their luggage for the transatlantic trip. The advice was probably passed on to later settlers, for the process of preparing homemade rennet was long and tedious. The basic ingredient was a fresh calf's stomach—difficult enough to obtain in the New World—an essential ingredient for it contained rennin, the enzyme needed to coagulate milk into cheese.

The stomach was first pickled in brine, then salted, dried, and cut into small pieces, which were kept tightly closed in a container. In addition to its use in producing sage and cheddar cheese, the most popular varieties of the period, rennet was also needed for turning milk into curds.

In producing curds, rennet was added to a large quantity of milk to produce a sour liquid called clabber. After several hours, the curds or crumblike particles of fat and protein separated from the watery whey. Next the curds were tied in a cloth and allowed to drain. The chilled, dry curds were eaten with cream as a breakfast dish, or as a dessert with sugar and nutmeg.

A selection of several desserts was customary at meals in the homes of wealthier families. Along with their main sweet, rich New England merchants and southern planters also sampled a selection of various dainties. These secondary desserts often included macaroons, prunes, glazed almonds, sugared raisins, quinces, sweet relishes, and sliced fresh fruit.

Colonial women, untrained in the professions or for jobs as artisans, frequently supported themselves by selling their home-cooked desserts. Early newspapers include numerous advertisements for the public sale of fresh cakes,

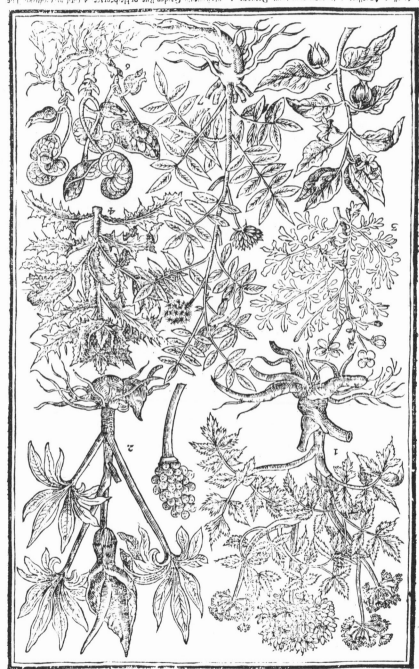

Angelica; Dragons; Garden Rue, or Herbegrace; The blessed Thistle; Winter Cherries; Asarabacca; Licoris, by John Parkinson. English, woodcut, 1629. Courtesy The Garden Library, Dumbarton Oaks, Washington, D.C.

puddings, pies, and jellies straight from the kitchens of private homes. Even large roasts or sides of animals too large to be prepared in certain homes were cooked by these amateur chefs for their clients. This type of industriousness was one of the few socially acceptable methods for widows or independent young women to earn their livelihood. Some, however, restricted their sales to various weekly markets where farmers also hawked their goods.

Most seventeenth- and eighteenth-century desserts can be prepared as final touches to today's space-age dinners. For those who do not have a spare calf's foot handy, gelatin can be substituted and the elegant flummery recipe does not suffer significantly.

Pennsylvania German cake mold of carved wood showing tulip design. Eighteenth-century style. *Courtesy National Gallery of Art, Index of American Design.*

Dessert Recipes

CAKES

TO MAKE CHEESECAKE WITHOUT CURD Beat two eggs very well; then put as much flour as will make them thick. Then beat three eggs more very well, and put to the other with a pint of cream, and half a pound of butter. Set it over the fire, and when it boils put in your two eggs and flour, and stir them well, and let them boil till they be pretty thick. Then take it off the fire, and season it with sugar, a little salt, and nutmeg; put in currants, and bake them in pattipans as you do others.

The Compleat Housewife, 1730

TO MAKE GINGERBREAD CAKES Three pounds of flour, a grated nutmeg, two ounces ginger, one pound sugar, three small spoons pearl ash dissolved in milk, one pound butter, four eggs. Knead it stiff, shape it to your fancy. Bake fifteen minutes.

New American Cookery, 1805

TO BAKE MOLASSES GINGERBREAD One table spoon of cinnamon, some coriander or allspice, put to four teaspoons pearl ash dissolved in half pint water, four pounds flour, one quart molasses, four ounces butter. (If in summer rub in the butter, if in winter, warm the butter and molasses and pour into the spiced flour) knead well till stiff, the more the better; the lighter and whiter it will be; bake brisk fifteen minutes. Don't scorch; before it is put in, wash it with whites and sugar beat together.

American Cookery, 1796

AN ORDINARY CAKE TO EAT WITH BUTTER Take two pounds of flour, and rub into it half a pound of butter; then put to it some spice, a little salt, a quartern and a half a half of sugar, a half a pound of raisins stoned, and half a pound of currants. Make these into a cake with half a pint of ale-yeast, and four eggs, and as much warm milk as you see convenient. Mix it well together, an hour and half will bake it. This cake is good to eat with butter for break-fast.

The Compleat Housewife, 1730

TO MAKE PLUM CAKE   Mix one pound of currants, one drachm nutmeg, mace, and cinnamon each, a little fat, one pound citron, orange peel candied, and almonds bleach'd, six pounds of flour (well dry'd) beat twenty one eggs, and add with one quart new ale yeast, half pint of wine, three half pints of cream and raisins.

American Cookery, 1796

TO MAKE POTATOE CAKE   Boil potatoes, peal and pound them, add yolks of eggs, wine and melted butter, work with flour into paste, shape as you please, bake and pour over them melted butter, wine and sugar.

New American Cookery, 1805

TO COOK SPONGE CAKE   Take ten eggs, one pound of sugar, one half pound of flour; beat the yolks, sugar and flour together.

The Husbandman and Housewife, 1820

COOKIES AND CANDY

TO CANDY ANGELICA   Take angelica that is young, and cut it in fit lengths, and boil it till it is pretty tender, keeping it close covered. Then take it up and peel off all the strings; then put it in again and let it simmer and scald till 'tis very green; then take it up and dry it in a cloth and weigh it, and to every pound angelica, take a pound of double-refined sugar beaten and sifted.

Put your angelica in an earthen pan, strew the sugar over it, and let it stand two days. Then boil it till it looks very clear, and put it in a colander to drain the syrup from it, and take a little double refined sugar and boil it to sugar again. Then throw in your angelica and take it out in a little time, and put it on glass plates. It will dry on your stone or in an oven after pyes are drawn.

The Compleat Housewife, 1730

TO CANDY ANY SORT OF FLOWER Take your flowers and pick them from the white part. Then take fine sugar and boil it candy high. Boil as much as you think will receive the quantity of flowers you do, then put in the flowers and stir them about till you perceive the sugar to candy well about them. Then take them off from the fire, and keep them stirring till they are cold in the pan you candied them in. Then lift the loose sugar from them, and keep them in boxes very dry.

The Compleat Housewife, 1730

TO MAKE MACAROONS Take a pound of almonds, let them be scalded, blanched and thrown into cold water, then dry them in a cloth and pound them in a mortar. Moisten them with orange-flower water, or the white of an egg, lest they turn to an oil. After, take an equal quantity of fine powdered sugar with three or four whites of eggs, and a little milk; beat all well together, and shape them on wafer paper with a spoon. Bake them on tin plates in a gentle oven.

The Frugal Housewife, 1772

TO PREPARE PEPPERMINT DROPS Pound and sift four ounces of doubly refined sugar, beat it with the whites of two eggs till perfectly smooth; then add sixty drops of oil of peppermint, beat it well, and drop on white paper, and dry at a distance from the fire.

A New System of Domestic Cookery, 1807

TO BAKE CHRISTMAS COOKEY To three pounds flour, sprinkle a tea cup of fine powdered coriander seed, rub in one pound butter, and one and half pound sugar, dissolve three teaspoons of pearl ash in a tea cup of milk.

Knead all together well, roll three quarters of an inch thick, and cut or stamp into shape and size you please. Bake slowly fifteen or twenty minutes; tho' hard and dry at first, if put into an earthen pot and dry cellar, or damp room, they will be finer, softer and better when six months old.

American Cookery, 1796

TO MAKE MARCH-PANE   Take a pound of Jordan almonds, blanch and beat them in a marble mortar very fine. Then put to them three quarters of a pound of double-refined sugar, and beat with them a few drops of orange-flour water. Beat all together 'til a very good paste, then roll it into what shape you please. Dust a little fine sugar under it as you roll it to keep it from sticking.

To ice it, searce double-refined sugar as fine as flour, wet it with rose-water, and mix it well together, and with a brush or bunch of feathers, spread it over your march-panes; bake them in an oven that is not too hot; put wafer-paper at the bottom, and white paper under that, to keep them for use.

The Compleat Housewife, 1730

CHEESE

TO MAKE CHEDDAR CHEESE   Take the new milk of twelve cows in the morning and the evening cream of twelve cows, and put to it three spoonfuls of rennet; and when 'tis come, break it, and whey it; and when 'tis well whey'd, break it again, and work into the curd three pounds of fresh butter, and put it in your press, and turn it in the press very often for an hour or more and change the cloths, and wash them every time you change them.

You may put wet cloths at first to them; but towards the last put two or three fine dry cloths to them, let it lie thirty or forty hours in the press, according to the thickness of the cheese; then take it out and wash it in whey, and lay it in a dry cloth till 'tis dry; then lay it on your shelf, and turn it often.

The Compleat Housewife, 1730

TO MAKE SAGE CHEESE Your curd must be prepared in the same manner as for the common cheese, and squeeze out as much of the juice out of sage and spinnage as will give it a fine greenish colour. Put it to the curd, with which it must be properly mixed, then put it into the mould, and press it in a moderate manner, and it will eat very agreeably at the expiration of about six months.

New American Cookery, 1805

CREAMS, CUSTARDS, FOOLS

TO MAKE QUINCE CREAM Take quinces, scald them till they are soft, pare them, and mash the clear part of them, and pulp it through a sieve; take an equal weight of quince, and double refin'd sugar beaten and sifted, and the whites of eggs and beat it till it is as white as snow, then put it in dishes.

The Compleat Housewife, 1730

TO PREPARE RASPBERRY CREAM Take a quart of thick sweet cream, and boil it two or three wallops; then take it off the fire, and strain some juice of raspberries into it to your taste. Stir it a good while before you put your juice in, that it may be almost cold when you put it to it, and afterwards stir it one way for almost a quarter of an hour; then sweeten it to your taste, and when it is cold, you may send it up.

The Frugal Housewife, 1772

TO MAKE ALMOND CUSTARD Take a pint of cream, blanch and beat a quarter of a pound of almonds fine, with two spoonfuls of rose-water. Sweeten it to your palate. Beat up the yolks of four eggs, stir all together one way over the fire, till it is thick; then pour it out into cups. Or you may bake it in little china cups.

The Frugal Housewife, 1772

TO MAKE BOILED CUSTARD Put a stick of cinnamon to one quart of milk, boil well, add six eggs, two spoons of rose-water, bake.

American Cookery, 1796

GOOSEBERRY FOOL Pick the stems and blossoms from two quarts of green gooseberries, put them in a stew pan with their weight in loaf sugar and a very little water; when sufficiently stewed, pass the pulp through a sieve, and when cold, add rich boiled custard till it is like thick cream; put it in a glass bowl and lay frothed cream on top.

The Virginia Housewife, 1825

TO MAKE ORANGE FOOL Take the juice of six oranges and six eggs well beaten, a pint of cream, a quarter of a pound of sugar, a little cinnamon and nutmeg. Mix all together, and keep stirring over a slow fire, till it is thick, then put in a little piece of butter, and keep stirring till cold, and dish it up.

The Art of Cookery, 1747

FLUMMERY Take a large calfs foot, cut out the great bones, and boil them in two parts of water; then strain it off and put to the clear jelly half a pint of thick cream, two ounces of sweet almonds, and an ounce of bitter almonds, well beaten together. Let it just boil, and then strain it off, and when it is cold as milk from the cow, put it into cups or glasses.

The Frugal Housewife, 1772

TO MAKE A WHIPPED SYLLABUB Take two porringers of cream, and one of white wine, grate in the skin of a lemon, take the whites of three eggs, sweeten it to your taste, then whip it with a whisk. Take off the froth as it rises, and put it into your syllabub glasses or pots, and they are fit to use.

The Frugal Housewife, 1772

PIES AND TARTS

TO MAKE POTATOE PASTY   Boil, peel, and mash potatoes as fine as possible; then mix pepper, salt and a little cream, or if you prefer, butter. Make a paste, and rolling it out like a large puff, put the potatoe into it and bake it.

A New System of Domestic Cookery, 1807

TO MAKE AN APPLE OR PEAR PIE   Make a good puff paste crust, lay some round the side of the dish. Pare and quarter your apples and take out the cores, lay a row of apples thick. Throw in half the sugar you design for your pie, mince a little lemon peel fine, throw over and squeeze a little lemon over them, then a few cloves, here and there one, then the rest of your apples and the rest of your sugar.

You must sweeten to your palate, and squeeze a little more lemon. Boil the peeling of the apples and cores in fair water, with a blade of mace, till it is very good. Strain it and boil the syrup with a little sugar, till there is but very little and good, pour it into your pie, put on the upper crust and bake it. You may put in a little quinee or marmalade, if you please.

The Frugal Housewife, 1772

TO MAKE DRIED APPLE PIE   Take two quarts dried apples, put them into an earthen pot that contains one gallon, fill it with water, and set it in a hot oven, adding one handful of cranberries: after baking one hour, fill up the pot again with water; when done and the apples cold, strain it, and add thereto the juice of three or four limes, raisins, sugar, orange-peel and cinnamon to your taste. Lay in paste.

New American Cookery, 1805

TO MAKE POTATOE PIE   Scald one quart milk, grate in four large potatoes while the milk is hot, when cold, add four eggs well beaten, four ounces butter, spice and sweeten to your taste. Lay in paste. Bake half an hour.

New American Cookery, 1805

TO FIX GOOSEBERRY TARTS Lay clean berries and sift over them sugar, then berries and sugar, till a deep dish be filled, intermingling a handful of raisins, and one gill of water; cover with paste, and bake somewhat more than other tarts.

Grapes must be cut in two and stoned and done like a gooseberry.

New American Cookery, 1805

TO BAKE CARROT PUDDING A coffee-cup full of boiled and strained carrots, five eggs, sugar and butter of each two ounces, cinnamon and rose-water to your taste, baked in a deep dish without paste, one hour.

New American Cookery, 1805

A BOILED FLOUR PUDDING One quart milk, nine eggs, nine spoons flour, a little salt, put into a strong cloth and boil one and a half hour.

New American Cookery, 1805

TO MAKE POTATOE PUDDING One pound boiled potatoes, one pound sugar, half a pound butter, ten eggs.

The New England Cookery, 1808

A TASTY INDIAN PUDDING Three pints scalded milk, seven spoons fine indian meal, stir well together while hot, let stand till cooled; add four eggs, half pound raisins, four ounces butter, spice and sugar. Bake four hours.

New American Cookery, 1805

TO COOK A BOILED RICE PUDDING Take a quarter of a pound of rice, and a half a pound of raisins stoned. Tie them in a cloth so as to give the rice room to swell. Boil it two hours. And serve it up with melted butter, sugar, and grated nutmeg thrown over it.

The Frugal Housewife, 1772

A BOILED SUET PUDDING Take a quart of milk, a pound of suet shred small, four eggs, two spoonfuls of grated ginger, or one of beaten pepper, a teaspoon of salt. Mix the seasoning and suet first in one pint of milk, and make a thick batter with flour. Then mix in the rest of the milk with the seasoning and suet till it becomes a pretty thick batter. Boil it two hours. Serve it up with plain butter.

The Frugal Housewife, 1772

TO MAKE A TRIFLE Cover the bottom of a dish or bowl with Naples biscuits broke in pieces, macaroons broke in halves, and ratafia cakes. Just wet them all through with sack; then make a good boiled custard, not too thick, and when cold pour it over it. Then put a syllabub over them. You may garnish it with ratafia cakes, currant jelly and flowers.

The Frugal Housewife, 1772

TO MAKE A WHITPOT Cut half a loaf of bread in slices, pour thereon two quarts milk, six eggs, rose-water, nutmeg, and half a pound sugar; put into a dish and cover with paste. Bake slow one hour.

New American Cookery, 1805

TO PREPARE AN EXCELLENT AND CHEAP DESSERT DISH Wash a pint of small hominy very clean, and boil it tender; add an equal quantity of corn meal, make it into a batter with eggs, milk and a piece of butter. Bake it like batter cakes on a griddle, and eat it with butter and molasses.

The Virginia Housewife, 1825

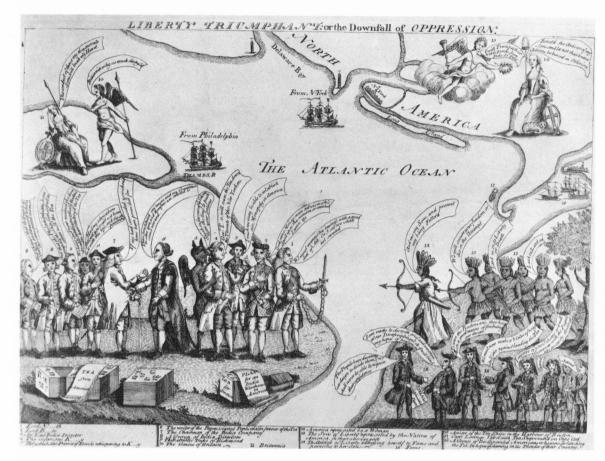

Liberty Triumphant: or The Downfall of Oppression. English engraving, 1774. *Courtesy Colonial Williamsburg, Williamsburg, Virginia.*

Beverages

In perhaps one of the greatest gastronomical feats ever recorded, a mug of chocolate quaffed with pickled oysters was breakfast fare for Virginia gentleman William Byrd in the early eighteenth century. Later, he altered the menu to a more digestible one of sausage and chocolate.

Although most settlers did not choose such tasty combinations, chocolate was a popular drink for all ages. The beverage was simple to prepare for the imported cocoa beans were merely ground and then brewed to the desired thickness with water or milk.

As America moved further into the eighteenth century, chocolate and coffeehouses became popular in seaport towns such as Boston, New York, and Philadelphia. Perhaps professional expertise in preparing these drinks was sorely needed for many were unsure of exactly what to do with the newly imported beans. In some Boston homes, the ritual of consuming coffee originally involved eating the boiled beans and then drinking the liquid coffee. Some unknowing settlers when first confronted with tea, ate the stewed tea leaves with butter and threw away the liquid tea as a waste product.

The taste of coffees, teas, and chocolates was unpredictable at best. Today's beverages are a smooth blend of leaves or beans of many types. However, in colonial times, a ship's cargo usually included not a mixture of several strong and mild beans, but only the products of a single plantation. Past experiences with the crop of a particular producer were of little value in judging later shipments, for changing climatic and soil conditions altered the tastes of a particular grower's crop from year to year.

In larger cities, prominent merchants may have blended different varieties of beans or teas into pleasing mixtures, but for the most part, the taste of a

Three types of early American drinking vessels. *Left:* wooden or treen mug; *center:* seventeenth-century leather bottle; *right:* brown salt-ware jug dated 1643. *Courtesy The Smithsonian Institution.*

beverage was discovered only after a cup had been brewed in the home. Almost every housewife had a particular private method for drying, roasting, and brewing coffee, but in most instances a raw egg, shell and all, was added to the grounds before boiling.

When coffee was not available or was beyond the means of the poorer family, parched rye, chestnuts, or grape seeds were substituted for coffee beans and brewed into hot drinks. The use of these less than prime grounds may have contributed to the habit of calling coffee the essence of old shoes or syrup of soot.

Tea substitutes were also popular, particularly on the frontier where imported merchandise was difficult to purchase. Sassafras tea was considered particularly pleasing and was highly valued in Europe. In the old countries, the beverage was considered a remedy for almost any illness and for syphilis in particular. The search for sassafras is considered by some to be a major factor in the settlement of South Carolina, an area where the plant supposedly grew profusely.

In 1596, Nicholas Monardes proclaimed the amazing curative powers of sassafras in his book *Joyfull Newes Out of the New-Found Worlde:*

It may bee three yeeres, pass, that I had knowledge of this Tree, a Frenchman which had beene in those parts, shewed me a peece of it, and told me meruels of the Vertue thereof, how many and variable diseases were healed with the water which was made of it . . . He told me that the French men, which had beene in the Florida at that time, when they came into those parts, had beene sicke the most of them, of grievous and variable diseases, and that the indians did then shown them this tree, and the manner how they should eat it, and so they did and were healded of many evilles . . .

Monardes, however, doubted many of the miraculous claims of the New World explorers: ''. . . in these things of Plantes, and hearbes which are brought from other places, they say much, and knowe little, unless it be by a man that hath experience of them with care and diligence.''

America's abundant tea-drinking habits confounded many foreign visitors. Swedish traveler Per Kalm suggested that the overindulgence of tea-drinking by American women was a direct factor in causing their teeth to fall out before the age of twenty.

Colonial tea addicts were sorely tested when the nationwide tea strike began about ten years before the Revolutionary War. Supporters of the boycott

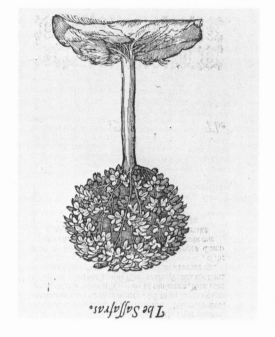

The Sassafras, by Nicholas Monardes. English, woodcut, 1596. Courtesy The Garden Library, Dumbarton Oaks, Washington, D.C.

against British tea published numerous testimonials by patriotic doctors who claimed that tea-drinking not only shortened the life of a drinker, but weakened his spleen and stomach. Other disastrous side effects were tremors, spasmodic infections, general weakness, and permanent effeminacy, evidently a claim aimed at producing dreaded fear among colonial men.

High prices as well as patriotism discouraged many from drinking tea. The price of tea per pound in Boston soared from four to eleven shillings between 1768 and 1769.

Rhubarb, goldenrod, strawberry, and blackberry leaves were also collected for brewing into tea during the long show of solidarity against the British. The later revolution saw a great decrease in the amount of American tea-drinking, and in the first years of the new republic, coffee became the overwhelming favorite drink. Though never to regain its prewar popularity as a general beverage, tea remained popular as a medicinal home remedy for various illnesses, a turnabout from the boycott claims to the opposite effect.

Excessive is probably the best word to describe the alcoholic drinking habits of early colonists. In every section of the country, even the most routine meeting or task was considered due cause for a nip of brew. Harvests, lawsuits, house-raisings, elections, and even business deals were signaled with profuse drinking. Even in staid New England, where public drunkenness caused considerable consternation, the consuming of alcoholic beverages was part of the settler's routine homelife.

Public taverns were not only inns to shelter the wayside traveler, but served to satisfy the thirsts of local residents. In New Amsterdam by the mid-1600s, it was estimated that one out of every four buildings was a place in which either brandy, tobacco, or beer was sold.

Women were particularly active as proprietors of inns and taverns, perhaps because the establishments could be run in conjunction with normal housekeeping activities. From 1762 until the outbreak of the Revolution, nearly 750 licenses for operating taverns were issued to women in Pennsylvania alone. The figure is more than 20 percent of all those approved. Scores of other women probably engaged in the business without bothering to secure a license. Many of these female keeps also provided food and benefited from the custom that travelers nearing the tavern at dinnertime would try to bag a deer or other game as his contribution to the meal.

Spirits flowed particularly free on royal birthdays, holidays, and family celebrations, when even small children consumed heavily of cider, wines, and liquors. The aspiring political candidate paid dearly for this friendly custom, for both lavish tables of food and numerous kegs of drink were expected at the polling places to compensate travel-weary voters who often rode many miles to cast their ballots.

In the Virginia election of 1758, candidate George Washington's bill included charges for 146½ gallons of rum punch, beer, wine, and brandy, all for only a few hundred voters. Washington, however, won the election.

Tavern sign. American, painting on wood. *Courtesy National Gallery of Art, Index of American Design.*

Fifteen years later, delegates to the Continental Congress in Philadelphia took the time out from their serious deliberations to sample both the local hospitality and brew. John Adams described these gatherings in a 1774 letter to his wife Abigail :

We go to congress at Nine, and there We stay, most earnestly engaged in Debates upon the most abstruse Misteries of State untill three in the Afternoon, then We adjourn, and go to Dinner with some of the Nobles of Pensylvania, at four O Clock and feast upon ten thousand Delicacies, and sitt drinking Madeira, Claret and Burgundy till six or seven, and then go home, fatigued to death with Business, Company and Care . . . I drink no Cyder, but feast upon Phyladelphia Beer, and Porter.

Colonists drank for many reasons, the first being Old World tradition. It was part of the English custom to refuse water in favor of great quantities of cheap beer and ale. French and Spanish settlers were used to their wines, while German and Dutch pioneers in the colonies had been weaned from an early age on schnapps.

Tavern sign. American, painting on wood. *Courtesy National Gallery of Art, Index of American Design.*

Secondly, settlers drank because they did not maintain even the most basic sanitary precautions or refuse disposal. Water resources near villages were often garbage filled, polluted, or perhaps frozen over during winter. Many colonists attached medicinal qualities to liquor and felt that a glass of alcohol at different times of the day would help to ward off diseases such as malaria.

Finally, days in the New World were filled with dangers, cold, and hunger. Death often came at an early age and personal disasters were part of life. Spirits helped the colonists to carry these ever present burdens and made existence in the harsh wilderness more cheerful. For whatever reason, colonists were ready to drink almost anything that could be squeezed, diluted with water, and fermented.

Yet a major problem faced the thirsty ones who desired alcoholic spirits. The ships coming to America had no room for transporting numerous casks of liquor. Those that were brought most often did not survive the difficult passage without extensive damage to the flavor. This same problem arose years later on the western frontier after breweries had been established in coastal

Portable liquor carrier, made to be carried on horseback. American, late eighteenth century. *Courtesy National Gallery of Art, Index of American De-sign.*

Ship and Turtle tavern sign. American, painting on wood, 1806. *Courtesy The Shelburne Museum, Inc., Shelburne, Vermont.*

cities, but transportation of heavy kegs was difficult over the narrow foot-paths that served as roads. As a result, wild fruit trees and cultivated apple orchards provided the means for homemade beverages.

Hard cider was the most popular drink and was available at all times of the day; it was served in a cold tankard at breakfast and as a warm toddy at bedtime. Many a man's worth was measured by the number of cider barrels in his private store and the casks were often willed to the most favored child. One village of forty families is recorded as having on hand more than three thousand barrels of cider during 1721, a testimonial to the popularity of the drink. Although much of this was undoubtedly sold in nearby towns, the efforts and orchards required to produce this quantity are vast even by today's standards. Applejack, a brandy made from cider, was almost as popular as an everyday drink. Perry was made by the same process as was cider, but with the juice of pears rather than apples.

Beer has been a part of the American scene since the early days when settlers believed the beverage was necessary to maintain good health. The cura-tive powers of colonial beer are not verifiable, but a widely held belief was that the brew was a preventative for scurvy. Sailors on ocean voyages and residents in northern areas where fresh fruits and vegetables were not always available drank huge quantities of beer for the prevention of this dread disease. Any benefits were often offset by a deadly disease called the dry gripes. European brewers customarily included massive doses of lead-based additives to preserve their beer during the trip to America. Effects were swift for hundreds of unfortunate beer drinkers who quickly died from lead poisoning.

Large amounts of beer were consumed at both the lowest and highest economic levels. Students at Harvard College paid a portion of their tuition in wheat and malt, which was then used to supply the brewhouse maintained by the school.

Early beers were generally classified as strong, middling, or small, de-pending upon their alcoholic content and method of brewing. The ingredients used in the preparation of beer included locally grown grains such as barley, wheat, oats, rye, and wild hops, as well as a limited amount of imported malts. Many home brewers, however, substituted other products of nature for the traditional grains. Among the beers widely consumed were those made from pine chips, spruce, hemlock, fir, birch, apple skins, sassafras, pumpkins, Jerusalem artichokes, and persimmons. Poorer families produced beer from molasses and bran, while ginger beer, a product of these times, survives today as a popular beverage.

Stringent regulations were often placed on the manufacture and sale of beer. Dionis Coffin, who kept a tavern in Newbury, Massachusetts, was one colonial who believed in the theory that citizens can fight city hall and win. When she was called before the local court in 1653 on a charge of selling beer above the legal price, she retaliated. Dionis, obviously proud of her brew, brought in witnesses who swore that she used finer ingredients than the law required. The court relented and allowed the higher charge.

Stronger drinks such as ale and porter, an eighteenth-century invention combining three types of malts, were imported into the colonies. Like imported beer, however, these products were drunk less frequently than the cheaper domestic types.

Cherries, blackberries, elderberries, persimmons, currants, and mulberries provided the makings for homemade wines and cordials, but many of these beverages were not produced by the poor because of the large amounts of sugar needed in their manufacture.

By the late seventeenth century, increased merchant shipping put imported wines and brandies within the price range of even the large middle class. Inland southerners were now able to purchase, at reasonable cost, wines from the Canary or Azores island groups. Lisbon sack or sherry was readily available to the northern citizen, as were French clarets, burgundies, and champagnes. It was not unusual to find private cellars with more than three hundred bottles of a mixed stock.

French Huguenots were brought to Virginia to oversee planting of grapevines in 1610, and by 1624 the general assembly of Jamestown decreed that every freeman's garden of from one-quarter to one acre should include at least twenty grapevines for wine. During the next century, a public vineyard of two hundred acres was established at Williamsburg, supervised by French wine makers and worked by community-owned slaves. The venture was evidently not successful, for in 1777 both the slaves and the land were sold.

Grapevines from Germany's Rhine area were reported to have been flourishing in Pennsylvania in the mid-1700s and were sent to Massachusetts by Benjamin Franklin for planting there. But most American wines were not held in highest favor by the general public, who elected to imbibe stronger liquors. In Old Salem, North Carolina, a combination brewery, distillery, and tavern owned by the Moravian Church listed more than fifteen hundred gallons of whiskey, brandy, rum, and cognac in the inventory of their public tavern. Only sixty gallons of wine were recorded.

Wine bottle dated 1737 excavated from
a refuse pit in Virginia. *Courtesy
The Smithsonian Institution.*

Silver tankard. American, eighteenth
century. *Courtesy National Gallery of
Art, Index of American Design.*

While wines, cider, brandies, and cognacs were drunk straight, mixed drinks were also extremely popular. Ratafias were made by combining straight spirits with fruit concentrates. Possets involved a sweet cream or milk base that had been curdled with liquor. Metheglin was a part medicinal, part pleasure drink made of honey, spirits, and herbs. A popular punch named sangree was prepared from wine mixed with water and then spiced or sweetened. On cold days a common item was caudle, a drink made from hot ale or wine that had been mixed with eggs, bread, sugar, and spices.

Hard liquor cocktails such as blackstrap, a mixture of rum and molasses, aggravated the already chaotic custom of public health-drinking. This exchange of pleasantries, which has not altogether disappeared, was occasioned most often in taverns and inns. Basically, each drinker in the inn's common room toasted the health of each other drinker present. A separate toast was required for each guest and by etiquette the toasts were followed with great gulps of liquor. This practice led to excessive inebriation, particularly if the inn was crowded, or the drinking mugs were large.

Because all the drinkers were toasting each other simultaneously, the common rooms of these inns were often places of mass confusion, great shouting, and general drunkenness by the time the last toast had been made. Many travelers who were strangers were forced to constantly repeat their names and business to friendly locals who wished to drink their health.

Toasting was also an important part of the drinking ritual outside the tavern environment. A custom in the most elegant homes called for children to be given a glass of wine before dinner with which to toast their parents' health.

John Fontaine, the official chronicler of an expedition led by Virginia Governor Alexander Spotswood, detailed the particular colonial custom of toasting and firing guns as a method of celebration. In his diary, Fontaine described the near riotous scene that took place as the governor's expedition reached its destination at the top of the Blue Ridge:

We had a good Dinner, and after it we got the Men together, and loaded all their Arms, and, we drank the King's Health in Champagne, and fired a Volley—the Princess's Health in Burgundy, and fired a Volley—and all the Rest of the Royal Family in Claret, and a Volley. We drank the Governor's Health and fired another Volley. We had several Sorts of Liquors, VIZ., VIRGINIA Red Wine and White Wine, IRISH Usquebaugh, Brandy, Shrub, two Sorts of Rum, Champagne, Canary, Cherry, Punch, Water, Cider, ETC.

Sea Captains Carousing in Surinam, by John Greenwood. American, oil on bed ticking, 1758. *Courtesy City Art Museum of Saint Louis.*

Domestic and imported whiskies began to be rivaled about 1670 by the manufacture of New England rum or kill-devil. Although the operation was strongly condemned by Quakers and other abolitionists, many new fortunes were established in the famous trading triangle.

Under this scheme, merchants purchased slaves on the African coast using rum as payment. The slaves were then transported to sugar plantations in the British West Indies in the same ships that had brought the rum to the dark continent. In the Caribbean islands, the slaves were traded for molasses that had been locally produced. The cargo of molasses was then loaded into the same empty vessels and shipped to New England, made into rum, which in turn was sent back to Africa for the purchase of more slaves, and the triangle began again.

This rum trade became so important that a major part of the New England economy was endangered by Parliament's passage of the 1733 Molasses

Slaves cultivating the Sugar-cane.

Slaves cultivating a field of sugarcane. Woodcut. *Photo courtesy Library of Congress.*

Act. The bill, which imposed a duty of sixpence per gallon on foreign molasses imported directly into the colonies, resulted in smuggling becoming a major practice of American shippers. Although the protests of New England merchants helped to reduce the tariff to threepence thirty years later, the smuggling was only slightly slowed. Illegal traffic continued for many years in products such as Spanish sherries and wines.

African slaves, who formed such an important part of the trading triangle, were involved in colonial alcohol during the earliest part of American history. Records indicate that among the first blacks brought to this country were those who were paid partially in liquor. In 1581, Negro slaves of the Spanish king were sent to Saint Augustine to help construct artillery platforms. While white workers were compensated with small money payments, blacks received only bread, meat, and wine.

This policy of payment in drink changed significantly, however, as slavery became more widespread and the threat of black revolt became imminent.

By the eighteenth century, most English colonies had set strict fines of up to thirty pounds for the sale of strong drink to slaves. In some areas, limited amounts of whiskey could be given to blacks or Indians, but only in cases of physical distress or to relieve pain. Despite these restrictions, drinking of hard liquor was evidently as widespread among Negroes and Indians as it was among white settlers.

The production of alcoholic beverages by Indians in prerevolutionary times was probably limited to a light persimmon beer mentioned by Captain John Smith in his early writings. Eighteenth-century accounts of everyday

The Prodigal Son Reveling with Harlots. Artist unknown. American, watercolor, late eighteenth century. *Courtesy Abby Aldrich Rockefeller Folk Art Collection, Williamsburg, Virginia.*

life do mention that Indians produced wines from corn and various fruits, but it is not clear if this was done because of old tribal custom or if the practice was copied from the brewing habits of white settlers.

Atlantic coast Indians appear to have been more moderate manufacturers of drink than their western cousins who produced alcohol from many types of plants such as cactus and mesquite. Despite their ingenuity, however, Indian production of alcohol never approached the sophisticated level of white colonials.

Rooster weathervane, reported to be from the old Fitch Tavern in Bedford, Massachusetts (near Concord). American, painting on wood, c. 1775. It was here the Minutemen rallied on the morning of April 19, 1775. *Courtesy The Shelburne Museum, Inc., Shelburne, Vermont.*

Beverage Recipes

TO CURE A BUTT OF ROPY BEER Mix two handfuls of bean flour with one handful of wheat flour and stir in.
The Husbandman and Housewife, 1820

TO MAKE SPRUCE BEER OUT OF SHED SPRUCE To one quart of shed spruce, two gallons of cold water, and so in proportion to the quantity you wish to make. Then add one pint of molasses to every two gallons, let it boil four or five hours and stand till it is luke warm. Then put one pint of yeast to ten gallons, let it work, then put into your cask and bring it up tight, and in two days it will be fit for use.
New England Cookery, 1808

TO MAKE CAUDLE Make a fine smooth gruel of half grits; strain it when boiled well, stir it at times till cold. When to be used, add sugar, wine and lemon peel, with nutmeg. Some like a spoonful of brandy besides the wine.
A New System of Domestic Cookery, 1807

TO MAKE CHERRY BRANDY To every four quarts of brandy, put four pounds of red cherries, two pounds of black and one quart of raspberries, a few cloves, a stick of cinnamon and a bit of orange-peel. Let these stand a month, close stopped, then bottle it off, put a lump of sugar in every bottle.
The Compleat Housewife, 1730

TO MAKE COFFEE MILK Boil a dessert spoonful of ground coffee, in nearly a pint of milk, a quarter of an hour; then put into it a shaving or two of isinglass and clear it. Let it boil a few minutes and set it on the side of the fire to grow fine.
A New System of Domestic Cookery, 1807

RYE COFFEE   Wash rye in several waters to free it from dust, blighted grain, etc. Boil it in water until some of the grain cracks open, then drain it, and dry it in an oven, then burn it as other coffee. Barley is said by some to be superior to rye for making coffee, and is prepared in the same way.

The Husbandman and Housewife, 1820

TO MAKE CURRANT WINE   Take four gallons of currants, not too ripe and strip them into an earthen stean that has a cover to it. Then take two gallons and a half of water and five pounds and a half of double refined sugar. Boil the sugar and water together and scum it, and pour it boiling hot on the currants and let it stand forty-eight hours. Then strain it thro' a flannel bag into the stean again and let it stand a fortnight to settle and bottle out.

The Compleat Housewife, 1730

TO MAKE HYDROMEL OR MEAD   Mix your mead in the proportion of thirty-six ounces of honey to four quarts of warm water; when the honey is completely held in solution, pour it into a cask. When fermented, and become perfectly clear, bottle and cork it well.

If properly prepared, it is a pleasant and whole drink, and in summer particularly grateful on account of the large quantity of carbonic acid gas, which it contains. Its goodness, however, depends greatly on the time of bottling, and other circumstances which can only be acquired by practice.

The Virginia Housewife, 1825

TO FIX LEMONADE   To be made the day before wanted. Pare two dozen tolerably sized lemons as thin as possible, put eighteen of the rinds into three quarts of hot, not boiling water, and cover it over for three or four hours. Rub some fine sugar on the lemons to attract the essence, and put it into a china bowl, into which squeeze the juice of the lemons.

To it add one pound and a half fine sugar, then put the water to the above, and three quarts of milk made boiling hot. Mix and pour through a jelly bag till perfectly clear.

A New System of Domestic Cookery, 1807

TO MAKE POSSET   Put a pint of good milk to boil, as soon as it doth so, take it from the fire and let it cool a little; and when it is pretty well cooled, pour it into the pot, wherein is about two spoonfuls of sack and four of ale, with sufficient sugar dissolved in them, so let it stand a while near the fire, till you eat it.

The Family Dictionary, 1705

TO MAKE A RATAFIA   Blanch two oz. of peach and apricot kernals, bruise and put them into a bottle, and fill nearly up with brandy. Dissolve half a pound of white sugar candy in a cup of cold water, and add to the brandy after it has stood a month on the kernals, and they are strained off; then filter through paper and bottle for use.

A New System of Domestic Cookery, 1807

TO MAKE RICE CREAM OR MILK   Take a quart of either of them, then put in two handfuls of rice flour, and a little fine flour, as much sugar as is fit, the yolk of an egg, and some rosewater.

The Family Dictionary, 1705

TO MIX SACK POSSET   Take ten eggs, beat the yolks and whites together and strain them into a quart of cream. Season it with nutmeg, cinnamon and sugar, put to them a pint of canary, stir them well together, put them in your bason, then set it over a chaffing dish of coals, and stir it till it be indifferently thick, then scrape on sugar and serve it.

The Family Dictionary, 1705

TO MAKE SHRUB   Take two quarts of brandy, and put it in a large bottle, adding to it the juice of five lemons, the peels of two, and half a nutmeg. Stop it up, let it stand three days, and add to it three pints of white wine, and a pound and a half of sugar. Mix it, strain it twice through a flannel, and bottle it up. It is a pretty wine and a cordial.

The New England Cookery, 1808

ECONOMY IN THE USE OF TEA   Save the tea leaves, dry them to a crisp, reduce them to a fine powder in a mortar; a teaspoon in a rag, put into a tea pot will be equal in quality and flavor to three spoonfuls of the tea leaves when first used.

The Husbandman and Housewife, 1820

TO MAKE BEEF TEA   Take lean beef, a pound, cut it in thin slices, put it into a quart of water, boil it a quarter of an hour: then take out the meat, mince it small and boil it a quarter of an hour more, skimming it well.

The Family Receipt Book, 1819

TO MAKE WINE OF BLACKBERRIES   Take and bruise the blackberries a little, then let them ferment for twenty-four hours, then put them into a barrel with a little tartar and a few ripe grapes, let the water just boil and stand till it be luke warm, and then put it to the blackberries.

The Family Dictionary, 1705

Glossary

A la mode—A dish cooked or served according to the most popular fashion of the times.

Ale yeast—A leavening agent used in cooking and produced as a by-product of ale-brewing.

Balls—Small round patties of minced or diced meat. Balls were usually highly seasoned, fried, and used for garnishing.

Balneo—A therapeutic solution of mineral waters.

Basin or Bason—A bowllike container in which food was served.

Bay Salt—Coarse salt crystals produced by the evaporation of seawater, usually by the heat of the sun.

Beard—To dress or remove the excess parts of food, usually applied to the cleaning of shellfish.

Bladder—Internal animal organs used as airtight coverings for pots or jars.

Boat—Any deep container used for serving liquids or stews and shaped like a boat.

Case—To skin for cooking; also to enclose, as sausage, in a protective coat.

Catsup—A liquid stock of vegetables or meats simmered with spices and herbs for long periods and then used as a flavoring in sauces. Also katsup. Can be made from either a tomato or water base.

Caudle, Coddle or Coudle—To cook or stir gently; also a warm alcoholic beverage.

Caul—To remove an enclosing membrane or layer of skin.

Chine—A cut of meat that includes any section of the backbone and adjacent flesh.

Cimlin—A variety of squash.

Collar—To prepare meat by rolling it into a coil and binding with a string. Also the neck sections of animals.

Crown—A piece of shortening or other ingredient cut into slices approximately the size of a large silver coin.

Cunners or Conners—Small perchlike fish from the Atlantic Ocean.

DO—An abbreviation for ditto.

Drachm—A dram; any small amount; as much as can be held in one hand.

Draw—To pull out the insides of an animal; also to flatten.

Faggot—Herbs or flavoring greens tied into a bunch.

Flannel—Material used as a sieve to strain liquids.

Flea—To skin or beat meat.

Flitch—A thick slice of side of meat; usually refers to smoked food such as bacon.

Forc'd meat—Highly seasoned meat that has been chopped fine and used for stuffing or "forcing" fowl.

Fricassee—A cooking method whereby food is cut into serving size pieces, then fried or stewed in its own gravy.

Froth—To heat to bubbling or to brown just before serving.

Gravy—Any broth or stock produced from boiling vegetables or meats with spices.

Haslet—The edible internal organs of animals.

Hung—Meat that has been suspended aboveground for curing; also game that has been left unattended so that it can become high, or slightly spoiled. This distinctive high taste of food was extremely popular during the colonial period.

Innards—All the internal parts of an animal.

Interlaced—To mix one ingredient into another in layerlike weaving patterns.

Isinglass—A gelatin-type adhesive, similar in function to egg whites, but prepared from the membranes of fish bladders.

Joil or Jole—The jaw or upper throat parts of fish and other animals, in cattle it is called the dewlap, and in fowl, the wattle.

Lard—Layers of pork fat or melted hog grease; also to stuff or mix pork into other meats.

Leather—Sections of animal skins used as airtight containers, covers, or bindings in food preparation and canning.

Leather up—To beat briskly.

Middling—Of medium or average size or strength. Also pork cut from the center portion of a hog.

Mold or Mould—To mix gently.

Neat—Any member of the bovine family, such as cows, oxen, or bulls.

Orange flower water—Liquid flavoring containing the aroma and taste of orange flowers.

Palates—Meat cuts that include the roof of an animal's mouth and throat. Also to season a dish according to taste.

Pasty—A pie or tart, usually containing meat filling and baked on a tin sheet.

Pearl ash—Potash mixed with other salts.

Pennyworth—Any small amount; as much as can be bought with a penny.

Petre-salt—Unrefined saltpeter.

Pot—To preserve, usually in a container; to cook in a crock.

Potage or Pottage—A thick stew or soup.

Potash—The alkaline residue left from burning certain vegetables or wood ashes in iron pots.

Powder or Pouder—To partially preserve by sprinkling with salt.

Q S—As much of an ingredient as is needed.

Ragout—A highly seasoned stew of meats and vegetables.

Rand—A long strip of meat; in beef, the section between the flank and the buttock.

Relish—A pleasing flavor.

Roche alum—The raw crystal fragments of sulfates used as an astringent in cooking.

Rosewater—Water flavored with the essence of roses.

Sal prunella or Prunella salt—Salt cakes made from burned saltpeter.

Salamander—Metal fireside implements; also a pan for browning.

Salmagundi—An assortment of various chopped foods.

Saltpeter—Salty crystalline substances used medicinally and in food preservation; a powder that gives a pleasing redness to preserved meats.

Scrag—A lean piece of meat such as a neck or back.

Search—A sieve or strainer.

Send it up—To serve a dish; to send the meal upstairs from the kitchen.

Sippets—Small pieces of toast or bread.

Suet—Crumbly fat around the kidneys and loins of cattle and sheep.

Swim—Food allowed to float around in a large pot while cooking.

Viands—Food; usually the most choice items.

Verjuice or Verijuice—The sour liquid from unripened fruit such as cranberries.

Wallop—To boil vigorously.

Bibliography

Adams Family Correspondence. Edited by L. H. Butterfield. Vol. 1. Cambridge: The Belknap Press of Harvard University Press, 1963.

Allen, Zachariah. "The Conditions of Life, Habits, and Customs of the Native Indians of America and their Treatment by the First Settlers," an address delivered before the Rhode Island Historical Society, December 4, 1879. Providence: Providence Press Company, 1880.

American Heritage Book of Indians, The. Editor in charge: Alvin M. Josephy, Jr. New York: American Heritage Publishing Company, 1961.

American Heritage Cookbook and Illustrated History of American Eating and Drinking, The. New York: American Heritage Publishing Company, 1964.

American Lady, An. *New American Cookery.* New York: D. D. Smith, 1805.

Andrews, Charles M. *Colonial Folkways.* New Haven: Yale University Press, 1919.

————. *The Colonial Period of American History: The Settlement.* Vol. I. New Haven: Yale University Press, 1964.

Antiques Book, The. Edited by Alice Winchester. New York: Bonanza Books, 1950.

Aptheker, Herbert. *Essays in the History of the American Negro.* New York: International Publishers, 1964.

Aresty, Esther B. *The Delectable Past.* New York: Simon and Schuster, 1964.

Autobiography and Other Writings of Benjamin Franklin, The. Edited by Frank Donovan. New York: Dodd, Mead and Company, 1963.

Aykroyd, W. R. *The Story of Sugar.* Chicago: Quadrangle Books, 1967.

Baron, Stanley. *Brewed in America; A History of Beer and Ale in the United States.* Boston: Little, Brown and Company, 1962.

Bennett, Lerone, Jr. *Before the Mayflower; A History of the Negro in America, 1619–1962.* Chicago: Johnson Publishing Company, Inc., 1962.

Birds of America. Editor in chief: T. Gilbert Pearson. Garden City, New York: Garden City Books, 1936.

Boorstin, Daniel J. *The Americans; The Colonial Experience.* New York: Random House, 1958.

Bradford, William. *Of Plymouth Plantation, 1620–1647.* New York: Alfred A. Knopf, 1963.

Brewington, M. V. and Dorothy. *Kendall Whaling Museum Prints.* Sharon, Massachusetts: Kendall Whaling Museum, 1969.

Brickell, John. *The Natural History of North Carolina.* Dublin: Printed by James Carson for the author, 1737.

Bridenbaugh, Carl. *Cities in the Wilderness; The First Century of Urban Life in America, 1625–1742.* New York: Alfred A. Knopf, 1960.

————. *Myths and Realities; Societies of the Colonial South.* Baton Rouge: Louisiana State University Press, 1952.

Brown, Alice Cooke. *Early American Herb Recipes.* Rutland, Vermont: Charles E. Tuttle Company, 1966.

Brown, John Hull. *Early American Beverages.* Rutland, Vermont: Charles E. Tuttle Company, 1966.

Bruce, Philip A. *Social Life in Virginia in the Seventeenth Century.* New York: Frederick Ungar Publishing Company, 1964.

Burling, Arthur and Judith. *Chinese Art.* New York: Bonanza Books, 1953.

Carson, Gerald. *The Polite Americans.* New York: William Morrow and Company, Inc., 1966.

Carson, Jane. *Colonial Virginia Cooking.* Charlottesville, Virginia: University Press of Virginia for Colonial Williamsburg, Inc., 1968.

Carter, Susannah. *The Frugal Housewife.* Boston: Edes and Gill, 1772.

Catesby, Mark. *The Natural History of Carolina, Florida and the Bahama Islands.* London: Printed for C. Marsh, 1754.

Cobb, Thomas R. R. *An Historical Sketch of Slavery from the Earliest Periods.* Philadelphia: T. J. W. Johnson & Company, 1858.

Cole, Ann Kilborn. *Antiques; How to Identify, Buy, Sell, Refinish and Care for Them.* New York: Collier Books, 1966.

Comparative Studies of North American Indians. Transactions of the American

Philosophical Society. Edited by Harold E. Driver and William C. Massey. Vol. 47, Part 2. Philadelphia: The American Philosophical Society, 1957.

Cooley, Henry Scofield. *A Study of Slavery in New Jersey.* Johns Hopkins University Studies in Historical and Political Science. 14th Series, IX–X. Baltimore: The Johns Hopkins Press, September and October, 1896.

Cotter, John L., and Hudson, J. Paul. *New Discoveries at Jamestown.* Washington, D.C.: U.S. Government Printing Office, 1957.

Craven, Wesley Frank. *The Southern Colonies in the Seventeenth Century, 1607–1689.* Baton Rouge: Louisiana State University Press, 1949.

De Crévecoeur, Hector St. John. *Letters from an American Farmer, and Sketches of Eighteenth-Century America: More Letters from an American Farmer.* New York: The New American Library of World Literature, Inc., 1963.

Dexter, Elisabeth Anthony. *Colonial Women of Affairs.* Boston: Houghton Mifflin Company, 1931.

Diary and Autobiography of John Adams. Edited by L. H. Butterfield. Vol. 1, Diary, 1755–1770. Cambridge: The Belknap Press of Harvard University Press, 1961.

Diary of Samuel Sewall, The. Edited by Harvey Wish. New York: G. P. Putnam's Sons, 1967.

Dolan, J. R. *The Yankee Peddlers of Early America.* New York: Clarkson N. Potter, Inc., 1964.

Douglas, Marjory Stoneman. *Florida: The Long Frontier.* New York: Harper & Row, 1967.

Dow, George F. *Everyday Life in the Massachusetts Bay Colony.* New York: Benjamin Blom, 1967.

Driver, Harold E. *Indians of North America.* Chicago: The University of Chicago Press, 1968.

Dummond, Dwight L. *Anti-Slavery: The Crusade for Freedom in America.* Ann Arbor, Michigan: University of Michigan Press, 1961.

Earle, Alice Morse. *Child Life in Colonial Days.* New York: The Macmillan Company, 1962.

————. *Colonial Days in Old New York.* Detroit: Reissued by Singing Tree Press, 1968.

————. *Home Life in Colonial Days.* New York: The Macmillan Company, 1963.

Eaton, Clement. *A History of the Old South.* New York: The Macmillan Company, 1968.

Emerson, Lucy. *The New England Cookery*. Montpelier, Vermont: Printed for Josiah Parks, 1808.

Family Receipt Book, The. 2d American ed. Pittsburgh; Randolph Barnes, 1819.

Fessenden, Thomas G. *The Husbandman and Housewife*. Bellows Falls, Vermont: Bill Blake and Company, 1820.

Fishel, Leslie H. Jr., and Quarles, Benjamin. *The Negro American; A Documentary History*. New York: William Morrow and Company, Inc., 1967.

Fisherman's Encyclopedia, The. Edited by Ira N. Gabrielson. Harrisburg, Pennsylvania: The Stackpole Company, 1958.

Flanders, Ralph Betts. *Plantation Slavery in Georgia*. Cos Cob, Connecticut: John E. Edwards, 1967.

Fleming, Thomas J. *One Small Candle: The Pilgrims' First Year in America*. New York: W. W. Norton & Company, Inc., 1963.

Furnas, J. C. *The Americans; A Social History of the United States, 1587–1914*. New York: G. P. Putnam's Sons, 1969.

Glasse, Hannah. *The Art of Cookery*. 2d ed. London: for the Author, 1747.

Gentleman's Progress; The Itinerarium of Dr. Alexander Hamilton. Edited by Carl Bridenbaugh. Chapel Hill, North Carolina: University of North Carolina Press, 1948.

Goodwin, Rutherfoord. *A Brief and True Report Concerning Williamsburg in Virginia*. Williamsburg: Colonial Williamsburg, Inc., 1959.

Gould, Mary Earle. *The Early American House*. Rutland, Vermont: Charles E. Tuttle Company, 1965.

Grant, Anne. *Memoirs of an American Lady*. New York: Samuel Campbell by D. G. Bruce, 1809.

Great American Gentleman, The; The Secret Diary of William Byrd of Westover in Virginia, 1709–1712. Edited by Louis B. Wright and Marion Tinling. New York: G. P. Putnam's Sons, 1963.

Great Slave Narratives. Edited by Arna Bontemps. Boston: Beacon Press, 1969.

Greene, Lorenzo Johnston. *The Negro in Colonial New England*. New York: Atheneum, 1968.

Holliday, Carl. *Woman's Life in Colonial Days*. New York: Frederick Ungar Publishing Company, 1922.

Hume, Ivor Noël. *Here Lies Virginia; An Archeologist's View of Colonial Life and History*. New York: Alfred A. Knopf, 1963.

Johnson, Gerald W. *Our English Heritage*. Philadelphia: J. B. Lippincott, 1949.

Josselyn, John. *New-Englands Rarities.* London: Printed for G. Widdowes, 1672.

Lady, A. *The American Domestic Cookery.* Baltimore: Fielding Lucas, Jr., 1822.

Langdon, William Chauncy. *Everyday Things in American Life, 1607–1776.* New York: Charles Scribner's Sons, 1937.

————. *Everyday Things in American Life, 1776–1876.* New York: Charles Scribner's Sons, 1949.

Lathrop, Elise. *Early American Inns and Taverns.* New York: Tudor Publishing Company, 1935.

Leighton, Ann. *Early American Gardens; for "Meate or Medicine."* Boston: Houghton Mifflin Company, 1970.

Leonard, Eugenie A. *The Dear-Bought Heritage.* Philadelphia: University of Pennsylvania Press, 1965.

Life Treasury of American Folklore, The. By the editors of Life. New York: Time Incorporated, 1961.

Lincoln, Waldo. *Bibliography of American Cookery Books, 1742–1860.* Revised and enlarged by Eleanor Lowenstein. Worcester: American Antiquarian Society, 1954.

Lynes, Russell. *The Domesticated Americans.* New York: Harper & Row, 1963.

McColley, Robert. *Slavery and Jeffersonian Virginia.* Urbana, Illinois: University of Illinois Press, 1964.

McCormick, Richard P. *New Jersey from Colony to State, 1609–1789.* Princeton: D. Van Nostrand Company, Inc., 1964.

Miller, John C. *Origins of the American Revolution.* Boston: Little, Brown and Company, 1943.

Monardes, Nicholas. *Joyfull Newes Out of the New-Found Worlde.* 3d ed. Translated by John Frampton Marchant. London: E. Allde by assigne of B. Norton, 1596.

Morgan, Edmund S. *Virginians at Home.* Williamsburg; Colonial Williamsburg, Inc., 1962.

Narratives of Early Maryland, 1633–1684. Edited by Clayton Colman Hall. New York: Barnes and Noble, Inc., 1959.

New Jersey; A Guide to its Present and Past. Federal Writers Project. American Guide Series. New York: Hastings House, 1955.

Offbeat History: A Compendium of Lively Americana. Edited by Bulkey S. Griffin. Cleveland: The World Publishing Company, 1967.

Ogburn, Charlton, Jr. "The Passing of the Passenger Pigeon," *American Heritage,* vol. XII, June, 1961, p. 30.

Oxford English Dictionary, The. New York: Oxford University Press, 1961.

Parkinson, John. *Paradisi in Sole, Paradisus Terrestris.* London: H. Lownes and R. Young, 1629.

————. *Theatrum Botanicum.* London: T. Cotes, 1640.

Pennsylvania. Federal Writers Project. New York: Oxford University Press, 1940.

Phillips, Ulrich B. *American Negro Slavery.* Baton Rouge: Louisiana State University Press, 1966.

Priestly, Herbert I. *The Coming of the White Man, 1492–1848.* New York: The Macmillan Company, 1957.

Prose Works of William Byrd of Westover, The. Edited by Louis B. Wright. Cambridge: The Belknap Press of Harvard University Press, 1966.

Randolph, Mary. *The Virginia Housewife.* 2d ed. Washington, D.C.: Way and Gideon, 1825.

Ritchie, William A. *The Archaeology of Martha's Vineyard.* Garden City, New York: National Historical Press, 1969.

Rundell, Maria E. *A New System of Domestic Cookery.* Boston: William Andrews, 1807.

Rutman, Darrett. *Husbandmen of Plymouth; Farms and Villages in the Old Colony, 1620–1692.* Boston: Beacon Press, 1968.

Salmon, William. *The Family Dictionary: or Household Companion.* 3d ed. London: H. Rhodes, 1705.

Schlesinger, Arthur M. *The Birth of a Nation.* New York: Alfred A. Knopf, 1969.

Shepperson, Archibald B. *John Paradise and Lucy Ludwell of London and Williamsburg.* Richmond: The Dietz Press, Inc., 1942.

Simmons, Amelia. *American Cookery.* A facsimile of the 1796 first edition. New York: Oxford University Press, 1958.

Singleton, Esther. *Dutch New York.* New York: Benjamin Blom, 1968.

Smallzried, Kathleen Ann. *The Everlasting Pleasure, Influences on American Kitchens, Cooks and Cooking from 1565 to 2,000.* New York: Appleton Century Crofts, Inc., 1956.

Smith, E. *The Compleat Housewife; or, Accomplished Gentlewoman's Companion.* 4th ed. London: J. Pemberton, 1730.

Smith, John. *The Generall Historie of Virginia, New-England and the Summer Isles.* London: I. D. and I. H. for Edward Blackmore, 1632.

Society of Gentlemen, A. *The Universal Receipt Book.* New York: I. Riley, 1814.

South Carolina; A Guide to the Palmetto State. Federal Writers Project. American Guide Series. New York: Oxford University Press, 1941.

Stewart, George R. *American Ways of Life*. Garden City, New York: Dolphin Books, Doubleday and Company, Inc., 1954.

Stow, Millicent. *American Silver*. New York: Gramercy Publishing Company, 1950.

Tate, Thad W. *The Negro in Eighteenth Century Williamsburg*. Williamsburg: Colonial Williamsburg, Inc., 1965.

Treasury of Spices, A. Edited by Lester W. Jones. New York: American Spice Trade Council, 1956.

Trefethen, James B. "The Return of the White-Tailed Deer," *American Heritage*, vol. XXI, February, 1970, number 2.

Troup, Loris. *The Tasting Spoon; A Guide to Food Seasoning*. New York: The Citadel Press, 1955.

Tunis, Edwin. *Colonial Living*. Cleveland: The World Publishing Company, 1957.

Van Tassel, Valentine. *American Glass*. New York: Gramercy Publishing Company, 1950.

Ver Steeg, Clarence L. *The Formative Years, 1607–1763*. New York: Hill and Wang, 1968.

Virginia. Federal Writers Project. American Guide Series. New York: Oxford University Press, 1940.

Wertenbaker, Thomas Jefferson. *The Middle Colonies; The Founding of American Civilization*. New York: Cooper Square Publishers, Inc., 1963.

Wharton, James. *The Bounty of the Chesapeake; Fishing in Colonial Virginia*. Williamsburg: Colonial Williamsburg, Inc., 1957.

Willison, George F. *Behold, Virginia: The Fifth Crown*. New York: Harcourt, Brace and Company, 1951.

————. *The Pilgrim Reader*. Garden City, New York: Doubleday and Company, Inc., 1953.

————. *Saints and Strangers*. New York: Reynal and Hitchcock, 1945.

Wish, Harvey. *Society and Thought in Early America*. New York: David McKay Company, Inc., 1950.

Wittke, Carl F. *Who Built America*. New York: Prentice-Hall, Inc., 1964.

Woodson, Carter G., and Wesley, Charles H. *The Negro in Our History*. Washington, D.C.: The Associated Publishers, Inc., 1962.

Wright, Louis B. *The Cultural Life of the American Colonies, 1607–1763*. New York: Harper and Brothers, 1957.

————. *Everyday Life in Colonial America*. New York: G. P. Putnam's Sons, 1965.

Index